Relentless Mercy

Sermons

Lisa D. Kenkeremath

www.parsonsporchbooks.com

Relentless Mercy
ISBN: Softcover 978-1-949888-47-8
Copyright © 2017 by Lisa D. Kenkeremath

All rights reserved. No part of this book may be reproduced or transmitted in any form or by any means, electronic or mechanical, including photocopying, recording, or by any information storage and retrieval system, without permission in writing from the publisher.

Cover art: *The Good Samaritan (after Delacroix)* by Vincent Van Gogh, 1890. Kröller-Müller Museum, Otterlo, Netherlands. Used with permission.

All Scripture quotations are from the New Revised Standard Version unless otherwise noted.

To order additional copies of this book, contact:

Parson's Porch Books
1-423-475-7308
www.parsonsporch.com

Parson's Porch Books is an imprint of **Parson's Porch & Book Publishers** in Cleveland, Tennessee, which has double focus. We focus on the needs of creative writers who need a professional publisher to get their work to market, **&** we also focus on the needs of others by sharing our profits with those who struggle in poverty to meet their basic needs of food, clothing, shelter and safety.

Relentless Mercy

Sermons

Contents

Introduction 9

Creative Mercy

"In the Beginning" 17
   Genesis 1:1 - 2:4a

Covenant Mercy

The Rainbow Covenant..25
   Genesis 9: 8-17

Love to the Loveless..29
   Hosea 11:1-11

Inscribed on the Heart...34
   Jeremiah 31:31-34

Incarnate Mercy

Real Christmas 41
   Luke 2: 1-20

The Light Coming into the World..46
   John 1:6-8, 19-28

Providential Mercy

A Meal Is Not Just about the Food.. 53
   Matthew 14: 13-21

Inclusive Mercy

Divine Economics 59
  Genesis 21: 8-21

Going to the Dogs 64
  Matthew 15: 21-28

In the Shadow of the Cross 68
  Matthew 21: 1-11, 27: 11: 54

The View from the Ditch...72
  Luke 10:25-37

Etiquette for the Kingdom of God..77
  Luke 14: 1, 7-14

The Merciful Judge

Relentless Mercy 85
  Matthew 18:21-35

Credited with Righteousness 91
  Genesis 15: 1-7, Romans 4: 13-25

No Condemnation 96
  Romans 8: 1-6

Mercy in the Face of Chaos, Loss, and Death

"Precious in My Sight" 103
  Isaiah 43:1-7, Luke 3: 21-22

God of the Living.. 107
  Luke 20:27-38

The Absence of Christ 111
    Luke 24:44-51, Acts 1:1-11

To Whom Shall We Go? 115
    John 6: 58-69

Prison Break 120
    Acts 16: 16-34

The Wideness of God's Mercy: The Question of Universalism

"This Is How God Loved the World" 127
    John 3: 1-17

Introduction - Relentless Mercy

> The quality of mercy is not strained;
> It droppeth as the gentle rain from heaven
> Upon the place beneath. It is twice blest;
> It blesseth him that gives and him that takes:
> 'T is mightiest in the mightiest; it becomes
> the throned monarch better than his crown:
> His sceptre shows the force of temporal power,
> The attribute of awe and majesty,
> Wherein doth sit the dread and fear of kings;
> But mercy is above this sceptred sway;
> It is enthroned in the hearts of kings,
> It is an attribute of God himself;
> And earthly power doth then show likest God's
> When mercy seasons justice.

(William Shakespeare, "The Merchant of Venice," Act IV, Scene I)

Mercy is the wellspring of the gospel. We are more likely to name forgiveness as the essence of the Christian proclamation: asked to summarize the gospel, a typical American Protestant is likely to respond with something like "Jesus died for me, so now my sins are forgiven." Yet forgiveness is not the whole of the gospel. The tendency of North American Protestant Christians to focus on personal forgiveness has the effect of reducing God's astounding magnanimity toward God's creation to a private transaction between God and the individual sinner. Forgiveness is one aspect of *mercy*, the defining quality of God's stance toward humanity.

The Bible sees the human predicament as larger than the need for forgiveness. It is worth noting that Paul rarely uses the word "forgiveness" to describe what God has done through Jesus Christ. Paul speaks of the Christ-event as a cosmic rescue operation: human beings have been snatched from their captivity in the dominion of sin and death and delivered into a new dominion of life, peace and righteousness. Paul and other New Testament writers describe a great exchange, effected by God in Christ, of one mode of being for another (infinitely better) mode of being. In mercy, God has reclaimed us as God's own, restoring to us our rightful inheritance.

Divine forgiveness, of course, is not to be understated; but one problem I see in reducing the gospel to forgiveness of sins is that in our current cultural moment the concept of forgiveness in general has been degraded and cheapened. True forgiveness is costly: it is the high price that is paid by the injured party for the sake of reconciliation with the one who has done the injury. It requires telling the truth about the injury that has been done, attesting to the gravity of the offense against the life, health, rights, or dignity of the injured one. In light of the sacrifice that genuine forgiveness entails, it is disturbing to note the emergence of a new cultural phenomenon: forgiveness pronounced by an uninjured party.[2] Only those injured have the moral right to declare or enact forgiveness.

Divine mercy is an encompassing love that understands human frailty in all its dimensions, spiritual, moral, and physical. God's mercy flows from God's knowledge that we are "dust." Mercy is God's sympathetic turning toward the human person,[3] the active face of God's compassion. Such compassion includes pity, a word or concept that is distasteful to many – few of us like the idea of being an object of pity – but is commensurate with biblical understandings of God. God has pity on us in our weakness, fallibility, and contingency, and this pity motivates mercy. God "hears the cry" (Ex. 3:7) of the poor and oppressed, takes pity on them and responds.

There is ample testimony in the Old Testament that mercy is intrinsic to God's nature: what makes God *God* is mercy. God, the Scriptures tell us repeatedly, is "gracious and merciful, slow to

---

[2] For example, the "forgiveness" pronounced by Penn State fans on assistant coach Jerry Sandusky, who had molested dozens of young boys. A contrasting example of costly forgiveness is the almost mind-boggling sacrificial mercy demonstrated by members of the Mother Emanuel AME Church, who declared their forgiveness of the race-motivated shooter Dylann Roof after his slaughter of their family members and brothers and sisters in Christ.

[3] Walter Kasper, *Mercy* (Mahwah, NJ: Paulist Press, 2014), 43.

anger and abounding in steadfast love." Mercy is an aspect of God's holiness: "I am God and no mortal, the Holy One in your midst, and I will not come in wrath" (Hos. 11:9). God's mercy is God's covenant faithfulness: God is faithful to the covenant even when human beings are not, for the sake of the covenant.

In the life and death of Jesus Christ, God's mercy extends to taking mortality into God's own being. God has done this to "keep the covenant in force" by fulfilling, through Jesus' self-giving life and death, the covenant responsibility human beings have abdicated.[4] The extravagance of divine mercy can be shocking, as in God's justification of the "ungodly" (Rom. 5:6), reminding us that God's ways are not our ways (Isa. 55:8). Such outlandish mercy, though, is in God's nature; as Keck has noted, "God is never more authentically and characteristically God than in rectifying [justifying] the ungodly."[5]

It would be reasonable at this point to ask why I do not simply use the word "grace" instead of "mercy." Grace, perhaps a larger category than mercy, encompassing as it does love, forgiveness, and generosity, is a majestic, freighted, *theological* word, and many see it as only an attribute or action of God -- yet we, too, are supposed to be gracious, as God has been gracious toward us. "Mercy" is something we more easily recognize here on the ground; in other words, we more readily acknowledge a *human* capacity for mercy (as Portia's speech in *The Merchant of Venice* demonstrates), so we more readily understand that we are to reflect God's mercy through our own merciful actions.

Mercy is an aspect of God's "goodness." Early in my ministry I met with a young woman who told me about her childhood of abuse at the hands of her brilliant, charming and widely-admired father. She said that a source of comfort to her then and as an adult was her knowledge that, even with the evil she was enduring, there

---

[4] Kathryn Tanner, "Justification and Justice in a Theology of Grace," *Theology Today* 55:4 (January 1999), 518.

[5] Leander E. Keck, *Paul and His Letters*, Proclamation Commentaries, ed. Gerhard Krodel (Philadelphia: Fortress Press, 1988), 114.

was still "a source of goodness in the world," someone whose mercy stands against all the unmerciful things human beings can do to each other. The knowledge of that goodness existing beyond us and for us can sustain us through the injuries, shocks, and betrayals of earthly life.

This brings us to an important consideration: the nexus between God's mercy and God's justice. Divine mercy cannot be construed separately from the question of justice, God's righteous opposition to evil. Justice and mercy are reconciled in the cross and resurrection of Jesus Christ, God acting in mercy to restore the divine-human relationship that has been violated by human indifference and cruelty. God in Christ, as one who stands "above and not under the demands of pure justice,"[6] acts in mercy to heal and restore the relations between God and humanity. God's justice is activated in *mercy*, as the poet George Herbert well understood: "His ancient justice overflows our crimes."[7]

The final victory of God's mercy over the world's injustice will be seen on the eschatological horizon: the resurrection of Jesus from the dead is the "first installment" on a promise God has made to all humanity. The triumph of divine mercy in Christ's resurrection, God's vindication of Jesus, is a promise to all innocent sufferers that they will be vindicated, too. Divine mercy will prevail.

In a world that we experience so often as indifferent, impersonal, competitive and cruel, we are crying out for signs of mercy: a word of forgiveness, a comforting touch, a gesture of sympathy, a move against injustice, grounds for hope. The Scriptures speak to us of a God who is not indifferent or apathetic, who "hears the cry" of the rejected, the fearful, the disconsolate, the alienated, and the guilty. We meet this God in Jesus Christ, who not only healed the sick and blessed the children, but also ate with sinners, forgave his enemies, refused to return violence with violence, and in his risen body

---

[6] Kasper, 51.

[7] "The Bunch of Grapes," in *George Herbert: 100 Poems*, ed. Helen Wilcox (Cambridge, UK: Cambridge University Press, 2016), 105.

welcomed and commissioned those disciples who had denied and deserted him.

In Marilynne Robinson's *Home*, Glory Boughton, a minister's daughter who has returned to her small Iowa hometown to care for her dying father, remembers her father's preaching:

> For her, church was an airy white room with tall windows looking out on God's good world, with God's good sunlight pouring in through those windows and falling across the pulpit where her father stood, straight and strong, parsing the broken heart of humankind and praising the loving heart of Christ.[8]

I love this description of the preaching ministry. It is what I hope to do in my own ministry: illuminate the ways in which our God, in mercy, bends down to us to touch, heal, and repair our broken hearts and broken world. I hope these sermons show some of the ways in which the gospel still speaks to our contemporary experience of fall and redemption, loss, change, and renewal.

The sermons included in this collection were preached to different congregations I served in interim pastorates over a period of about nine years. In choosing to organize this collection around a single theme, I have tried to suggest the contours of a biblical theology of mercy; however, there is nothing systematic about this presentation, and the reader is sure to note many gaps and omissions. These are simply snapshots of Sunday-to-Sunday preaching, generally following the Revised Common Lectionary, and I hope the reader will be forgiving.

I dedicate this book to the congregations of Idylwood Presbyterian Church in Falls Church, Virginia; Good Samaritan Presbyterian Church in Waldorf, Maryland; and Grace Presbyterian Church in Springfield, Virginia. These congregations have inspired me,

---

[8] Marilynne Robinson, *Home* (New York: Farrar, Straus and Giroux, 2008), 50.

encouraged me, and challenged me; most of all, they have attested to the work of God's mercy through the gift of the church, where the Spirit leads us to make mercy concrete in caring for each other and for the world.

Creative Mercy

The book of Genesis, probably a product of the Babylonian exile, begins with a magnificent affirmation of a generous Creator. The first two chapters describe the work of a God whose power and mercy are seen in the taming of chaos, the ordering of the universe, the creation of human beings in the Creator's own image, and the pronouncement that it is all "good." The entire created world is the object of God's love, concern, and mercy.

This sermon was preached in the aftermath of two deadly natural disasters in 2008, a cyclone which hit Myanmar and an earthquake in China.

"In the Beginning…"
Genesis 1:1 – 2:4a

Last year I read a funny but also insightful book called *The Year of Living Biblically*, by A. J. Jacobs. Jacobs is a Jew – or, as he says, he is "Jewish in the same way that The Olive Garden is an Italian restaurant."[9] He didn't grow up in a Torah-observant family, but he set out to spend a year trying to follow the Bible as literally as possible. It was a year of discovery for him. He dealt with the intricacies of the dietary laws and the prohibitions against wearing clothing of mixed fibers, as well as practices that most modern urban Americans would consider bizarre, such as blowing a ram's horn at the full moon, sporting a full, untrimmed beard, and carrying a staff. He also attempted to honor in his daily life the Bible's concrete teachings regarding tithing, forgiveness of debts, telling the truth, and loving your neighbor "as yourself."

Over the course of the year, Jacobs's spiritual journey took him to the Creation Museum in Kentucky, "the Louvre for those who believe God made Adam less than six thousand years ago from dust."[10] The museum's founders are an evangelical group called Answers in Genesis. The museum is quite impressive, Jacobs says, with animatronic displays showing cave girls romping in the shadow of *T. rex*es -- because, we're told, in the beginning, humans and dinosaurs lived together in harmony. After his conversations with astrophysicists and engineers on the museum staff, who are dedicated to such things as describing the ventilation system of the Ark and conjecturing about a change in the speed of light since the universe began (to explain a 6000-year-old universe), Jacobs leaves musing over the amount of misplaced intelligence, creativity and ingenuity that has gone into this project. I would say it another way: The Answers in Genesis folks are forcing the Bible to do something it was never meant to do.

---

[9] A.J. Jacobs, *The Year of Living Biblically: One Man's Humble Quest to Follow the Bible as Literally as Possible* (New York: Simon & Schuster, 2007), 4.

[10] Jacobs, 56.

Lisa D. Kenkeremath

The first people who ever read Genesis 1 were probably the Jews which had been exiled in Babylon. They were not interested in a scientific explanation of the origins of the universe – they were interested in knowing who was in charge of it. It looked to them for all the world like the Babylonian gods were in charge. After all, the claims of these so-called gods had been backed up by mighty armies thundering into Jerusalem, razing the Temple to the ground, and carting off the people into captivity. As if in answer to their despair, they heard, or recited, the majestic cadences of Genesis 1, with its glorious, transcendent affirmation of one sovereign God who created an orderly world, filled it with beauty and life, and pronounced it all "good."

The first chapter of Genesis, if you haven't noticed before, is *poetry*. I think the Apollo Eight astronauts had a deeper sense of what this book of the Bible is all about than the developers of the Creation Museum. As they viewed the distant Earth looking beautiful, blue, and fragile in the immensity of space, they read the first ten verses of Genesis. People all over the world heard these ancient words through NASA's crackly radio transmission.[11] Many of them must have been moved to a new sense of wonder: wonder that in the vast distances of outer space, most of which is still deeply mysterious to us in spite of all our advances in astronomy, the planet Earth *exists*, sustains an almost infinite variety of life forms, and somehow, in a way we will never be able to explain, was brought forth by a divine Creator, spoken into existence by the animating force the Bible calls God's spirit. And the Bible says that this world is an object of God's love and concern.

Did you notice as we read that God's acts of creation, at every step of the way, also involve acts of organization? Every act of creation is accompanied by some act of separation: light from darkness; waters above from waters below; separation of plants and animals into different kinds; separation of humans from other creatures. What was a "formless void" now has a distinct geography, days and nights and seasons, and millions of creatures, each occupying its

---

[11] Noted by Dan Clendenin, 12 May 2008 at www.journeywithjesus.net/Essays/20080512JJ.shtml.

own rightful sphere of operations. Everyone and everything has a place in the created order. It is a world of balance and harmony.

As Christians, we are very used to reading the Bible primarily as a story of sin and salvation. The story of Adam and Eve in the second and third chapters of Genesis does seem to set the stage for such a reading -- but I'm not at all sure that's how the Bible was read by the ancient Hebrews. It seems to me that an awful lot of the Bible is about God beating back the chaos, bringing order, law, and harmony where there has been disorder, lawlessness, and conflict. In Genesis One, God tames the surging primeval waters and establishes the world as a place that is safe for human existence. Without God, Genesis says, there would be only darkness and chaos. Human history in the Bible is the story of violence and disorder being repeatedly brought under control by God: slaves are released from captivity, a people is formed out of a scraggly tribe of nomads, exiles are brought home, and human sin in all its disorderly manifestations of greed, strife and envy is dealt with in the person of Jesus Christ. God's love is projected into the world through God's work of subduing what is violent, unruly, and threatening to life.

Genesis says that because of God's spirit hovering over the world, there is a certain orderly predictability to the world. We can rely on the return of spring, the sun rising each morning, the rain falling, because everything is held and ordered by the providential hand of God. And God has called the creation "good" – lovely, pleasing, and beautiful. Before the story of original sin, there was "original blessing" – God's determination that the world should be a place of abundance and delight, where humans and animals alike can enjoy the fruits of their labors.

All these affirmations bring us to a theological problem. Though our perspective is not that of the Biblical literalists, we cannot escape some uncomfortable questions this text raises for us. How are we to reconcile this poetic vision of an orderly, harmonious creation, the work of a God in love with the world he has made, with the devastating events of the last two weeks: first, the cyclone that hit land in Myanmar and then the earthquake in China – the senseless loss of thousands of lives, the devastation of families, the destruction of whole villages, the eradication of decades' worth of human labor? What connection can be found between the creative "wind from God" that swept over the waters "in the beginning" and the swath of destruction that has cut through large parts of East Asia? How can we affirm the "goodness" of the world when such things happen?

Far worthier theologians than I have struggled to answer this question, and perhaps no one has given a truly satisfactory answer. (Maybe we should put the question to the folks at the Creation Museum, since they have "Answers in Genesis," but I suspect they don't have a handle on this, either.) All I can offer is this: that God created the world out of a tremendous *freedom*, the freedom of love seeking concrete expression, and God has given some of that freedom to the world and its creatures. That means that human beings are free to do evil or to do good; to wage wars or to make peace; to act in love or in hate; to seek God's will or to rebel against it. In a similar way, there is also some "freedom" built into the structure of the universe. There is a place for randomness. Meteorologists have noted that weather patterns will follow a predictable cycle of events, but as the cycle completes it never quite returns to its starting point, but to a nearby point "within the same slowly rotating figure-eight configuration."[12] In that place where the pattern starts again, there is possibility for a variety of different outcomes, a place where "chaos and order intersect."[13]

God has not created an "out-of-the-box" universe. In providing for freedom, God has allowed for the possibility of events that threaten human well-being. However, disturbing this may be to us, it means that God has given us a world that is open to the future, a world with constantly multiplying possibilities.

---

[12] Based on the "Lorenz Pattern" observed by meteorologist Edward Lorenz and noted by W. Sibley Towner, *Genesis* (Louisville: Westminster John Knox, 2001), 20.

[13] *Ibid.*

It also means God's work of creation is never finished. God is constantly acting – even struggling – to bring order out of chaos, even the chaos that sometimes engulfs ordinary human lives.

In Wendell Berry's novel *Jayber Crow*, a turning point in the life of the title character is the great flood of 1937 that hit large sections of Kentucky. I grew up in Louisville, and every ten years or so the *Courier-Journal* would publish pictures of the city submerged in the floodwaters, and people would start reminiscing. Many people died in the flood, and there was massive loss of property. It took years for the city to return to normal. In Berry's novel Jayber is trying to make a new start in life. He is making his way toward Louisville on foot, but all means of access are cut off. All around him are surging, foaming waters, rushing currents carrying trees, furniture, pieces of houses, animals. This is what it was like, he says: **"The earth was without form, and void; and darkness was upon the face of the deep. And the Spirit of God moved upon the face of the waters."** It is at that moment that the young man feels his need and helplessness, his aloneness in the world. Without any idea of where he is going, he finally finds shelter in the state capitol building in Frankfort, along with a whole crowd of frightened, exhausted, cold, and hungry displaced people holding on to their few remaining possessions. Even in the midst of this devastation, order begins to reassert itself. Relief workers serve hot soup. Families gather together, and children are put to bed on cots. Jayber is young and resilient, and he is hopeful as he contemplates the spectacle of an "old life submerged and gone, the new not yet come."

> ...I knew that the same Spirit that had gone forth to shape the world and make it live was still alive in it. I just had no doubt. I could see that I lived in the created world, and it was still being created. I would be part of it forever. There was no escape. The Spirit that made it was in it, shaping it and reshaping it, sometimes lying at rest, sometimes standing up and shaking itself, like a muddy horse, and letting the pieces fly.[14]

---

[14] Wendell Berry, *Jayber Crow* (New York: Counterpoint, 2000), 83.

As we stand in wonder before the mystery of creation and consider the terrible tragedies of the past two weeks, the responses of novelists and theologians may seem inexcusably glib. I can only think of the Burmese and Chinese people who have been hit by those flying pieces.

But the Bible gives us a consistent picture of a God who does not give up on the world, who is bound to the creation – who is, in truth, in love with the world. We are inescapably bound up with that creation, and bound to our Creator, held fast in hands that will not let us go. And that is something we also can pronounce "good."

Idylwood Presbyterian Church
Falls Church, VA
May 18, 2008

Covenant Mercy

Covenant love, or *hesed*, God's steadfast love toward the people of God, is a leitmotif of the Bible. Its context is God's covenant with Israel – but before there was the covenant with Israel, God made a pledge of faithfulness to all humanity.

The sermon texts give us glimpses into the inner life of God – God's heartbreak over human violence and unfaithfulness – and God's decision to give people mercy instead of what they deserve. Jeremiah 31 explores God's re-creation of the covenant in human hearts.

The Rainbow Covenant
Genesis 9: 8-17

Is the rainbow enough for you? Is this shimmer of light and color in the heavens, this pledge of God's faithfulness to the world enough to wipe out the memory of what has gone before? Does a happy ending erase the horror of millions perishing as floodwaters swept over the earth? And does the rainbow make us somehow forget the serious intent of the story of Noah and the flood?

We don't often dwell on the deep seriousness of the flood story. In our popular culture, it has been recast as a charming story for children, an inspiration for nursery decorations and themed birthday parties. Anyone who has ever lived through a catastrophic flood is not likely to be enchanted by the details of this story. I doubt that those who were in New Orleans when the levees broke are able to look at the biblical story in quite the same way as they might have before the devastation of Katrina.

The question the real biblical story raises for most people is a chilling one: Would God really do this? Would God order the wholesale destruction of the inhabitants of the earth, no matter how wicked they were? I will just say at the outset that those so-called biblical interpreters who saw the inundation of New Orleans as God's wrath against the supposed immorality of the city have completely missed the point of the story, which was that literally everyone on earth except Noah was wicked – there weren't any innocent people.

From the biblical perspective, "Would God really do this?" might be the wrong question to ask. That is not the focus of the story. The question the Bible wants us to ask is "What are the conditions that result in such a catastrophe?"

We'll need to go back a couple of chapters to see what the problem was. Genesis 6 describes the situation of the world in the time leading up to the flood. "The earth was filled with violence," Genesis tells us. "All flesh had corrupted its ways on earth." What we see in that chapter is God coming to terms with the hostility of the human heart toward God and God's peaceful purposes. Everywhere God looks, there is murder and mayhem, rape and pillage, the conquest and subjugation of the weak by the strong. God looks at the world God has created and is sickened by all the violence. The evil heart of humanity has caused the broken heart of God.

It shouldn't take much imagination for us to see what the Bible is talking about. The earth is filled with violence now, too. Just open a newspaper and it is all there. We're still hearing fresh allegations of torture at Guantanamo. Suicide bombs continue to blow up in streets, restaurants and marketplaces all over the world. We hear shocking stories of child abuse and spouse abuse. There's a more subtle violence, too, the kind driven by our insatiable need for more conveniences, more entertainment, more things – a need that is burning up fuel and putting carbon in the air, leading to melting ice caps and rising sea levels. Our way of life is drowning out God's vision of a world that is clean and whole and harmonious. The earth is still filled with violence. We can assume that it still breaks God's heart.

So, the Bible is clear in its assessment of the conditions that result in catastrophe. But there is a second, crucial question the Bible wants us to ask: What has God done about the fractured world? The answer God gives is the rainbow. The rainbow is the sign of God's resolve to stick with us, with the whole created world, no matter what. "I establish my covenant with you, that never again shall all flesh be cut off by the waters of a flood…When the bow is in the clouds, I will see it and remember the everlasting covenant …between me and you and every living creature."

Both the flood and the rainbow are about God and the world making a fresh start together. It is all God's idea, of course, and the interesting thing about it is that nothing about human beings has changed. A few verses before our text today, God looks down at Noah building his little altar and making an offering on it and says, "I will never again curse the ground because of humankind, for the inclination of the human heart is evil from youth" (8:21). There is nothing that suggests to God that human beings will be different from now on: the only change is in the heart of God.

This is something of a theological stroke of genius on the part of the biblical writers – against all the classical theologies that tell us God is immutable, impassible, the "unmoved mover," the Bible talks about a change in God's heart. It's something we'll see in the Old Testament repeatedly: God drawing back from anger, God deciding to give people mercy instead of what they deserve, God opting for forgiveness rather than punishment. That is not just a New Testament phenomenon – the Old Testament is shot through with stories of God's tenderness toward God's maddening human creatures.

There is something else about the rainbow covenant you may have noticed: it is not just with human beings. God says, "I am making my covenant with you and with every living creature that is with you, the birds, the domestic animals, and every animal of the earth…, as many as come out of the ark." That includes the giraffes gliding across the Serengeti plain, the Gila monsters sunning themselves in the Sonoran Desert, the humpback whales sending their haunting melodies through blue Pacific waters. Everything that moves and breathes is part of the covenant.

It is a unilateral covenant God has made with us, but as with all covenants something is expected of both parties. Here, I think, we human beings are to uphold our part of the covenant by acting respectfully toward the non-human members of that covenant: to maintain the conditions that will continue to sustain them, to restrain ourselves from violence against the created world.

That is not to say that we can recover some lost innocence, some primeval harmony between us and the rest of the created world. We are still entangled in a sinful world. This may be a hard notion for us to grasp, because we are so used to thinking in individual terms. I know that I can choose not to pull a gun on people who anger me, not to embezzle money entrusted to me, not to sell drugs to children. I can also choose to recycle, drive less, and buy local products. But there are areas of life in which it is harder to choose, because, intentionally or not, I am part of structures and institutions that are unjust to the poor or hostile to the natural world. From the Bible's perspective, sin isn't restricted to certain individuals; it is something that corrupts a whole society.

We are not innocent. The good news is that God has taken the measure of the human heart, has seen our inclination toward violence, and has decided to stick with us anyway.

Lisa D. Kenkeremath

A couple of years ago I saw something I will always remember. My husband and I were driving up Interstate 81, returning from a vacation. It had been raining, but the sky was clearing in the east. Just off the interstate, there was a sight familiar to anyone who has ever traveled in the American South: three crosses on a hillside, a big one in the middle, two smaller ones on either side, erected as a monument to the cross of Jesus and the two criminals crucified with him. On this day, though, there was an added feature to this tableau: through the breaking clouds, and right over the three crosses, there was a rainbow, as clear and shining as any rainbow you will ever see. There is nothing remarkable in this, that's what nature does when sun and water get together -- but on this day, it was as though a picture had been painted in the skies showing what our story with God is all about.

Consider: All the hostility and violence humanity is capable of were unleashed in the death of Jesus on the cross. But that violent death marked the beginning of an even greater new start for humanity. The rainbow is God's promise to protect us from the worst consequences of our evil or misguided actions, and the cross is God's willingness to suffer at our hands in order to keep that promise. It is an improbable truce God has enacted with humanity: we do violence to God on the cross, and receive God's peace in return.[15]

So, to return to the original question: Is the sign of the rainbow enough? Even under the best of circumstances, life is precarious, and we human beings have awesome power to either protect or destroy it. But God has set the bow in the clouds as an enduring sign of God's good intentions toward us and every living thing, God's desire not to let us perish. Under that sign, we may learn to live with the freedom of those who know they are loved, and with the joyfulness that leads to peace.

Idylwood Presbyterian Church
Falls Church, VA
March 1, 2009

---

[15] Observed by Rowan Williams, Archbishop of Canterbury. I have lost the original reference.

Love to the Loveless
Hosea 11:1-11

It's the people you love the most who hurt you the most. The son or daughter who left home in fury and headed down a path of self-destruction that you were helpless to stop. The sister who can't forgive you for something thoughtless you said years ago. The grandson who used to be your favorite companion, but now never calls or writes. It is when our family relationships go wrong that we suffer the most.

The prophet Hosea knew what it was like to give your heart to someone who had the power to make it bleed. One day Hosea fell in love with a girl named Gomer. We don't know what made her special in his eyes. We don't know if she was beautiful, whether she told stories that made him laugh or secrets that made him weep. Whoever she was, though, she commanded his heart as no woman had before. Every time he looked at her, something happened inside him, and he knew he was hers, forever. So, they married and had three children together.

But then Hosea began to discover some disturbing things about her. He didn't want to believe his suspicions, but the evidence kept piling up. He began to wonder if the two younger children were even his. Pretty soon, he became convinced they were not.

Then Gomer left him. She walked out the door to run off with her new lover, a man who was able to buy her pearls and perfume and vacations in four-star hotels.

Hosea thought he wouldn't live through the experience, it hurt so much. He was so furious he could hardly see straight, but he couldn't forget her either. He felt sick every time he heard her name, but he couldn't stop seeing her smile, hearing her voice, feeling her touch. The thought of her unfaithfulness stabbed his heart. Why had she left him? He had been so good to her, showing her nothing but love and kindness and loyalty.

Then Hosea heard she'd fallen on hard times – that her lover had turned out to be as unfaithful as she was and had dumped her, leaving her destitute.

Hosea's brain was telling him to forget her, let her go, abandon her to the horrible fate she deserved. Whatever she was going through right now, she had it coming. The trouble was, his heart wouldn't listen, so he went after her. He tracked her down to a sleazy hotel room in the red-light district, paid her debts, and brought her home. His friends and relatives were shocked. They reminded him of the shame he was bringing on himself. They told him he was a fool, and they laughed at him behind his back. Hosea went before Gomer like a shield, bearing the shame and abuse that should have been hers. When he got her back home, though, he let her know that neither of them would be shared with others after that: he expected a commitment.

Hosea's wife didn't deserve his love, but that didn't make him stop loving her. He couldn't be true to his own heart and just leave her to her own devices. For Hosea, it was all about relationships. When he chose to stay in relationship with Gomer, he knew it was going to cost him. Love, for him, meant accepting a certain amount of pain. The tragedy, of course, was that Gomer herself was incapable of bearing the demands that love made on her.

It was Hosea's peculiar vocation to love someone who was herself loveless. Hosea thought long and hard about this odd and painful vocation of his. What could it mean? What was God trying to tell him through this bitter experience, and what could he tell others?

Scary things were going on in Hosea's country, the northern kingdom of Israel. Over a period of fourteen years, there had been six kings, and four of them had been assassinated. The nation to the north, Assyria, had become a military superpower that was getting ready to march toward Israel. Israel's leaders, in spite of all the warnings by prophets like Hosea and Amos, dealt with this threat by making foolish alliances with the kings of other nations who couldn't possibly save them. As the kings of Israel and their advisors courted the foreign rulers, they began worshiping their gods. Israel had brazenly and heartlessly spurned the love of her

God. In fact, Hosea tells us in chapter 4, they had become a loveless people, forsaking both God and their fellow Israelites.

> There is no faithfulness or loyalty, and no knowledge of God in the land.
> Swearing, lying, and murder, and stealing and adultery break out;
> Bloodshed follows bloodshed. (4:2)

For Hosea, it was all about relationships. He began to see connections between the tragic story of his marriage to an unfaithful wife and the story of God and God's people. Hosea's own feelings of wounded love gave him a glimpse into the very heart of God. What God was going through must be something like what he felt when his wife abandoned him to run after other lovers, men who would never be as good and faithful to her as her own husband. If he, an ordinary human being, hurt this much, what must God feel at being rejected by the very people God had loved above all others, the people God had tenderly cared for ever since those early days in the wilderness?

> "When Israel was a child I loved him, and out of Egypt I called my son."

Maybe, Hosea thought, the analogy of husband and wife didn't say everything. A wife, after all, had a life of her own before she met her husband. Maybe what was going on between God and Israel was also something like a rupture between a parent and a child. When he thought about it, Hosea saw that the people Israel didn't even exist as a nation before God called them and claimed them and made them God's own. Through all the years of their wilderness wanderings, God fed them and protected them like a mother, picked them up when they were injured and kissed their hurts away. God taught them with a tenderness and patience they had never known before.

Their ingratitude was so hard to understand. Was it simply a matter of forgetting? Or was it just too much to be loved so completely? Were the people of God, like Gomer, simply incapable of accepting the burden of a love so generous, so pure -- so uncompromising? Perhaps Israel was simply not capable of the self-surrender that is the only appropriate response to such love. It would mean giving up some of her autonomy among the nations, her ability to cut deals and make alliances like they did. It would mean putting all her trust in this one God whose mighty love asked only to be returned. That was the one thing Israel couldn't do.

Israel's resistance posed an awful dilemma for Israel's God. The people seemed to be bent on self-destruction. It would seem that there was nothing left to do but let them take the consequences and write them off for good.

And this is where Hosea gives us a glimpse of the inner life of God: "How can I give you up...O Israel? my heart recoils within me; my compassion grows warm and tender."

God is asking the question Hosea could have asked Gomer: "Did you think that I loved you as little as you have loved me?" God loves this misguided, self-seeking child so much that God simply chooses not to let the devastation reach its final conclusion. Israel will suffer, but will not be destroyed.

> "How can I give you up, O Israel...How can I hand you over?"

In these anguished words, the very heart of the gospel is exposed: God loves us so much that God refuses to give us up or give up on us, even when the case against us argues otherwise. In considering the future of the people Israel, God was confronted with agonizing alternatives: to execute judgment that would mean giving them up forever; or to look the other way, and make light of their rebellion. Either way, they would be gone, because a love that doesn't make any demands or require any response is soon treated as cheap.

The northern kingdom of Israel was eventually conquered by Assyria. The people endured great loss and suffering, but they were not destroyed. They came back "trembling...like doves," shaken and repentant, and were returned to their homes.

Seven centuries later, God's agonizing choice reached its climax in the person of a Messiah. All the divine love and sorrow and hurt and anger, over men and women who couldn't recognize or respond to the ardent and vulnerable love of God, took shape in the life of Jesus of Nazareth. In Jesus, God let us know once and for all of God's love for the loveless – a love strong enough to let the redemption of these loveless ones cost him everything.

As Hosea knew, it's all about relationships. All the heartlessness that men and women like us are capable of cannot end the relationship that God has started with us.

The poet William Blake said that we are put on earth for just a little while, so that we might "learn to bear the beams of love." Learning to bear the beams of love means accepting, over and over again, the invitation to come home, to the one whose passionate love continues to seek us, whose compassionate love will not let us go.

August 8, 2010
Ingleside at Rock Creek
Washington, DC

Inscribed on the Heart
Jeremiah 31:31-34

The heart is a mysterious organ. Physiologically speaking, it is just the pump that drives the circulatory system, but we know it's more than that, don't we? The heart is the engine of life itself, and we know that when the heart stops, that's it – life stops, the curtain falls. Evidently, "every creature on earth has approximately two billion heartbeats to spend in a lifetime. You can spend them slowly, like a tortoise, and live to be two hundred years old, or you can spend them fast, like a hummingbird."[16] The hummingbird has a heart the size of a pencil point, and it beats ten times a second to power its breathtaking aerial feats and its all-consuming drive for food and flight. The hummingbird lives only two years.[17]

Is the heart, then, just an engine? In the western world, we like to think poetically of the heart as the seat of the emotions, the thing inside us that can "grow" or "melt" or "break" as a result of our wonderful, difficult entanglements with each other. Of course, that's so unscientific – but there was a story in *The Washington Post* just a couple of months ago about a man who had an artificial heart. He was very grateful for it – he would have died many years ago without this wonder of technology – but he had changed since he got his new heart, he said. He doesn't feel strong emotions anymore, and he's lost a lot of his drive. Life feels…flat. Others with artificial hearts have reported a similar phenomenon. No one can explain why, but some think it might have something to do with hormones whose production or deployment is related to functions of the human heart. The heart is a mysterious organ.

In the ancient world, the heart was not thought of primarily as the seat of the emotions, but as the place where will and intentions are formed. Maybe it's not as big a difference as we might think – if my emotions are engaged, something may happen to change my will and intention as well. For example, if the liquid brown eyes of a

---

[16] Brian Doyle, "Joyas Voladoras," *The Best American Spiritual Writing 2005*, Ed. Philip Zaleski (Boston/New York: Houghton Mifflin, 2005), 44.

[17] Doyle, 43-44.

puppy in a shelter cause my "heart" to melt with compassion, a new will or intention may be formed in me and I may go home with a pet I hadn't planned on!

According to Jeremiah, Israel had a problem with its "heart." The problem was that Israel's heart had gone all hard and cold against God. They went through the motions of worshiping – in fact, they rather enjoyed bringing sacrifices to the Temple and were pleased with their own piety – but once they had taken care of these specifically religious duties, they went about their way doing whatever they pleased. The falseness of their worship was proved by their callous indifference toward the widows and orphans and the rest of the poor. On a national level, their faithlessness was a disaster, leading them to make some very foolish choices that set them up for invasion by Babylon.

You could blame their predicament on Babylonian expansionism, but that's not what Jeremiah is concerned about. His concern is with Israel, not Babylon, and what he sees is a nation that has lost its moorings. They knew God had made a covenant with them, way back in the days of the Exodus, and they were proud of their status as the covenant people. But somewhere along the line they'd started thinking that "covenant" meant privilege, not responsibility, and started taking God for granted. Many of their priests aided and abetted them in their blind unconcern for God's commandments, a string of false prophets assured them that God wouldn't let anything bad happen to them, and the king was mainly concerned with enlarging his palace.

It broke Jeremiah's heart to see both the leaders and the people running headlong to their destruction. He pleaded with them, he thundered against them, he appealed to their good sense and better nature, all to no avail. They were convinced that God would protect them no matter what they did, so they branded Jeremiah as a "wacko" and even a traitor. He clashed with the public authorities, got thrown into prison for a while, and was even threatened with the death penalty. In spite of all this, though, Jeremiah didn't close his own heart to the plight of his people. He kept trying to get through to them, because just as his own heart was breaking, he knew God's was, too. "I remember how you used to love me," Jeremiah heard God cry to the people. "You followed me in the wilderness, and you were holy to me (2:2-3). But now you've forgotten me and broken my commandments." The pain and disappointment of God echo through the words of Jeremiah.

As you know, the worst did happen. Jeremiah saw it all long beforehand: the invasion, the capture of Jerusalem by the Babylonian army, the burning of the city, the deportation.

Having his prediction come true gave Jeremiah no satisfaction. It shattered his heart to see what was happening. But he also trusted that God had no intention of giving up on God's people. Jeremiah had spent forty years predicting death and captivity, but when the calamity arrived, he sought words of comfort for the broken people.

There is just so much a human being can do. He can bring the people the word of God, but he can't make them listen. So, when Jeremiah had reached the limit of his own powers, when the worst had already happened, God stepped in.[18]

People had completely forgotten what the original covenant was about, so God decided to make a new covenant with them. From now on, God said, the covenant would not be something written on tablets or scrolls – it would be written on their hearts. Instead of being something *outside* of them, now, by the work of God's Spirit, the covenant would be *inside* them. Now, it's not as if the first covenant, the one given on Mount Sinai, was all about obedience to God's laws and this new one said those laws didn't matter anymore. No, God was going to do something that would make obedience *possible*. The new covenant would touch people's hearts in a way that the first one hadn't. Only God could make this happen, of course, and how God could cause divine will and intention to get *inside* of people so that disobedience would lose all its appeal, only God truly knows.

It has something to do with forgiveness, though. After the end of life as they knew it, there was no way back for the people except by the love and mercy of God. "I'll remember their sin no more," said

---

[18] "A prophet can give man a new word, but not a new heart. It is God who must give man a heart to know that He is God." Abraham Joshua Heschel, *The Prophets, Vol. I* (Harper Torchbooks, 1969), 128.

God, and that was that. It didn't mean nothing more was expected from God's people from now on — it just meant that the starting place for their renewal had to be God, and only God. There was nothing they could do for themselves by themselves, but from now on, they would know God in a new way. God had not changed, but suddenly their *hearts*, their stubborn, recalcitrant *hearts*, would be changed. It would be a subtle thing — nothing would look different on the outside, but on the inside a quiet revolution would be going on, as the Spirit stealthily inscribed God's law on human hearts, and they began to respond out of the sheer joy and relief of being forgiven. And out of the experience of God's forgiveness, a new knowledge of God would be born. With these new, transformed hearts, following God would come as naturally as breathing.[19]

What does it take to get a new heart? In the world of human things, a glance, a touch, a memory, an unexpected word of kindness…and something shifts inside, a hard shell cracks, and something fresh and tender blooms into life.

What does it take to get a new heart? A God who says, "I will remember their sin no more." A God who says, "I will be their God, and they will be my people." A God who stops at nothing, not even a cross, to let us know that in spite of everything we do to get on the wrong side of God, God's love is more powerful than our resistance.

A heart that God has written on will never be the same again. This change of heart may not be a matter of strong emotions; it may be simply a shift in inclination, so that seeking and doing the will of God becomes part of who we are.

How does it happen? Only the Spirit of God knows that. But it does happen. And when it does, I'm told, there is nothing more pleasing to the heart of God.

Good Samaritan Presbyterian Church
Waldorf, MD
October 17, 2010

---

[19] Walter Brueggemann, *Hopeful Imagination: Prophetic Voices in Exile* (Philadelphia: Fortress Press, 1986), 293.

Incarnate Mercy

In the Incarnation, God expressed the divine self through a human life. As much as the cross, the Incarnation is an act of self-sacrificial love: God descending from the untouchable realms of heaven to make a place, "pitch his tent," with human beings. Improbably, God has chosen to become "entwined" with us, taking on a human life with all its possibilities of struggle, suffering, and love.

Real Christmas
Luke 2: 1-20

Not long ago, I heard a re-broadcast of David Sedaris's now-famous story about working as a Christmas elf at Macy's. As the picture-taking elf, Sedaris's job was to snap photos of children sitting on Santa's lap, presumably whispering to him their desires for Christmas morning. Many of the children did not want to sit in Santa's lap; more than a few were frightened of the prospect. Sedaris remembered one child and her mother in particular. It was little Rachel's turn to approach Santa, and she was resisting. Sedaris waited with his camera while a tug-of-war between exasperated mom and tearful child ensued. Finally, the mother burst out, "Rachel, you get up there and sit on that man's lap and smile, or I'll give you something to cry about!"

Reflecting on what he had seen during his Christmas-elf experience, Sedaris said, "It wasn't about the child, or Santa, or Christmas"...It was about adults trying to create a picture of the world as it should be, in "a world they cannot make work for them ."[20]

Christmas seems to bring out the tendency in all of us to want to somehow make things perfect, even if just for a day. I am no exception. Every December my life feels out of control with all the things to do, but I am determined to be ready for Christmas, both spiritually and materially. In my mind, I won't be doing any frantic, last-minute shopping, the house will be not only clean but perfectly organized, the Christmas dinner will be memorable, there will be fresh flowers in the guest room for anyone staying overnight. By about December 20th I realize I am not going to make this goal, but I don't stop stressing about it until I get to church on Christmas Eve. Christmas will come whether I'm ready for it or not, and thank God for that.

Most of us, I think, carry around some picture in our heads of what Christmas should be like. Maybe it is based on wonderful

---

[20] From "Santaland Diaries," broadcast on National Public Radio every December.

Christmases we remember from our childhood or maybe it is a vision of a Christmas we have never had. I'm sure this picture varies quite a bit from person to person, but a "mash-up" of an American storybook Christmas might go something like this:

> It is a beautiful, clear, cold December day. There is snow on the ground but not on the roads. The family loads up the car with presents and a tree and drives out into the country. The children do not fight during the car ride. We come to a simple but charming cabin surrounded by evergreens near a picture-book town. We put up the tree and decorate it. Then we go to a pretty little New England-style church for the Christmas Eve service and we feel God's peace surrounding us; as we leave, snow is gently falling, and we walk home through it. The children go right to bed in their new Christmas pajamas, and we have hot toddies by the fire. On Christmas Day other family members come, presents are opened, and we share a delicious meal around an old oak table. The children are well-behaved, and none of the adults air provocative political opinions, start arguments, or dredge up stories of past resentments. Family ties are renewed, and everyone ends the day in a warm glow.

I don't know of anyone who has actually had a Christmas like this, but something like this seems to be the gold standard for Christmas in the popular imagination, fueled, no doubt, by the advertising and greeting card industries. It's funny how the storybook Christmas has such a hold on our imaginations. Most of the year, we are all too aware that the world doesn't bend to suit our desires, but at Christmas we harbor some hope that it will. At a minimum, we expect Christmas to be a time when our lives feel simple and untroubled and calm, yet at the same time full to bursting with joy, anticipation, and hope.

The fact is that Christmas happens every year in a world that is still an Advent world, which is to say imperfect, out of joint, riven by anxiety, struggle, and pain. Even if our own lives are running smoothly – which can never be more than a temporary situation – we have only to look at what is going on in the world to feel some cognitive dissonance around the Christmas season. How can we say, "Joy to the world, the Savior reigns," we wonder, when the news from almost everywhere is grim? This Christmas, Ebola still rages in West Africa, 132 schoolchildren and nine adults have just died in a savage terrorist attack in Pakistan, and the war in Syria continues to take its toll of both combatants and civilians, many of them children. Here in our country, the racial divide seems as deep as ever, with tragic consequences on both sides of the divide, but especially for African-American boys and young men. On this day when we focus on a baby, a world of suffering children is painfully present. The helplessness of the infant Jesus is a reminder of how vulnerable children are, everywhere.

Despite our nostalgia for Christmases past, either real or imagined, the world has never been any different. The very first Christmas was not as calm and untroubled as the Christmas cards would have us believe. I've heard Luke's Nativity story described as an "enchanting" or "bewitching" tale, a story calibrated to charm the socks off us every year. Luke's story is beautiful, it is true, but the world that was the setting for Luke's events was a hard world, especially for poor people like Mary and Joseph. Luke's Nativity story, by the way, begins not with Mary or Joseph or Jesus, but with Caesar Augustus, to make it clear that there was only one person who could bend the world to suit his desires. Consider the Holy Couple's trip to Bethlehem: it was at Caesar's behest that they had to take that 100-mile journey, on foot, to meet a somewhat pointless-seeming bureaucratic requirement that in order for a census to be taken, everyone had to register in their hometown. Imagine making such an arduous journey, nine months pregnant, just to fill out a form! As Tom Long has noted, Mary and Joseph are like poor people everywhere and at every time, "at the whim of whatever Caesar or mindless bureaucracy...happens to lash out in their direction."[21] As poor people, their lives are a series of precarious arrangements already, so what does it matter if Mary

---

[21] Thomas G. Long, "Living by the Word," *The Christian Century*, December 10, 2014, 21.

gives birth in a warm room with her mother and a midwife present, or in a stable 100 miles from home? The poor are used to such accommodations.

In every age, Christmas breaks into the world of poverty and homelessness, wars and brutality, sickness, aging and dying. Christmas, after all, is not only a divine event, but also an intensely human event, an event of flesh and blood, an extraordinary thing happening to a very ordinary man and woman who were just struggling to get along in their part of the world.

In John Updike's 1982 novel, *Bech Is Back*, Henry Bech, a Jew who has married an Episcopalian, observes his wife's upper-middle-class Protestant Christianity:

> Many of [her] crowd went to church, much as faithfully as they played tennis and golf and attended rallies to keep out developers. Yet their God, for all of His colorful history and spangled attributes, lay above Earth like a layer of icy cirrus, a tenuous and diffident Other whose tendrils failed to entwine with fibrous blood and muscle.[22]

The coming of Jesus into the world contradicts any notion of a God so remote and icy. In the Incarnation, God has chosen to become enmeshed in human life, with all its intractability, its tangle of difficult relationships, its regular outbreaks of violence, cruelty, and ordinary meanness, as well as its fragility, tenderness and beauty. God has chosen to become "entwined" with us, to let us know that we are not alone in a vast and sometimes frightening universe. God does not abandon us. We can't make the world work for us, we will continue to suffer losses and disappointments, but these things do not separate us from God.

I suspect that that you are all here tonight for a variety of reasons. Many of you are regular churchgoers already, and you wouldn't dream of being anywhere else on Christmas Eve. Others of you

---

[22] John Updike, *Bech Is Back* (New York: Alfred A. Knopf, 1982), 122-123.

have grown up in this church but have been away at college or starting new careers, so tonight may feel a bit like a homecoming, with all the conflicting emotions that homecomings often arouse. Some of you are struggling with the faith you grew up with, no longer sure you still believe. Still others of you have been dragged here by a parent or a spouse and would just like to get this thing over with. It doesn't matter tonight how little or how much you believe, or whether it was your idea or somebody else's for you to be here. Christmas comes whether we are ready for it or not, for God in Christ greets us here tonight.

The message of Christmas is that God is with us. In Jesus Christ, we meet a real God for the real world. God does not swoop down from heaven to rescue us from the harsher realities of life; instead, God has come alongside us, shared our condition, even to the point of death itself. God in Christ saves us now from our lonely, scared, isolated selves and will eventually fully redeem our tired, old world. Christmas, real Christmas, is not about a perfect holiday but about the stirring of human hope when we understand that God is in the world, that Christ comes again and again, into the most unlikely situations and the most imperfect Christmases.

Grace Presbyterian Church
Springfield, VA
December 24, 2014

The Light Coming into the World
John 1:6-8, 19-28

In my life as a Christian pastor, I sometimes meet people who have an interest in the Christian faith but stop short of actual belief. They will often say something like, "I wish I could believe – my life would be much easier if I had faith." I am never entirely sure what people have in mind when they say something like this. Are they saying that my life is easier than theirs? Since I am a member of the clergy, some people imply that I have a closer connection to the divine than "regular" people, so that if I ask God for something I am more likely to get it than they are. Most people have a less instrumental view of the faith than that, but sometimes it seems that people think of belief itself as a force – that people of faith may endure calamities and hardships but that they are not touched by them in the same way as nonbelievers. It is as if faith gives us a suit of armor that shields us from the shocks and blows of human existence.

I know plenty of Christians whose faith is not working for them all that well right now. Some of them are being treated for a serious illness. One of them lost a job that was not only her livelihood but a source of deep satisfaction and personal fulfillment. A couple I know lost two of their three children, little boys only seven and eight years old, to a terrible disease. I know of many Christian young people who have graduated from college or grad school, having worked hard and done all the right things, but are finding out that the good jobs they have been trained for have disappeared. And looking beyond the community I know, what about Christians in places like Pakistan and Iraq, where simply being Christian can be punishable by prison or death? There are many faith-filled people in homeless shelters and hospital beds, refugee camps and disaster relief sites. Can we say that faith is making their lives easier?

If our faith is not making our lives easier, it is reasonable to ask, as nonbelievers sometimes do, what brings us here to worship every Sunday morning? Is it a conviction that if only we *believe*, God will fulfill our hopes? Deliver us from our troubles? Fight our battles and defeat our enemies? Take away our pain? If we believe, can we tap into divine power to make our dreams come true? What is the content of our religious expectations?

Most of us have been disappointed by life often enough that we would not say that our faith always works for us. So, what do the Gospels say?

Today's Gospel says that once "there was a man named John. He came as a witness to testify to the light."

If we stick to the Gospel readings for the Sundays of Advent, we cannot get away from John the Baptist. Every year at this time we hear that same voice crying from the wilderness, calling sinners to repent and warning of terrible times to come if they do not. But this week we see John a different way. He is not the fiery preacher clothed in camel skin and feeding on locusts in the desert; he is not even "the Baptist" here. He is simply a witness. He is here to tell us about something, to point us to something. John makes no claims for himself – in fact, he keeps insisting that he is nothing special, not the Messiah, not Elijah, not even "the prophet." He is not the light, the Gospel tells us, but he has come to testify to the light. The light, John says, is already here: "Among you stands someone whom you do not know."

When you put it that way, it has the effect of bursting the bubble of religious expectations. A political Messiah, a wonderworker like Elijah, a prophet who speaks words of timeless truth – those are people you can hang some expectations on. But what does a light do? A light enlightens. A light reveals. A light exposes untruth and reveals truth. A light can startle you, overturn your expectations. You may think you know what you want, but a light can show you what you need. "The light, the true light that enlightens everyone," John's Gospel says, "is coming into the world." And the light is not governed by our wishes. The light certainly does not depend on our belief.

That is the difference between the gospel and religion as we commonly understand it. Religion, to put it somewhat crassly, too easily turns into an attempt to get God on our side: to get God to work for us. Those who say they are "spiritual but not religious," by the way, are not immune to this error; the "spiritual" person may not look to get God on her side, but may believe that she can unleash some secret energy of her own soul to achieve a desired result. This is just a different twist on the idea of faith "working for" us. The gospel does not promise that Jesus will work for us. It promises that he will bring us light. The Gospel says, "Among you stands one whom you do not know." Well, we know him and we don't – or we think we know him and then we find him challenging our religious expectations. Someone like that cannot be the product of our own belief.

Belief itself has no power to do anything or change anything. I'm bemused every year by the Macy's holiday ad campaign. The slogan, emblazoned at the top of their newspaper ads and in the stores, is simply "Believe." I don't know what we are supposed to believe. That this Christmas will be different from all the others? That there really will be peace on earth? That we will get a diamond necklace, a cashmere coat, or a high-end watch, from Macy's? Macy's doesn't say. It just implies that *believing* will make your dreams come true.

Let's hear the Gospel again: "There was a man sent from God…to testify to the light…The true light, that enlightens everyone, was coming into the world."

John does not testify to an idea or a belief but to a person. This person alone, the one John calls the Light, can show us what we need. He alone can reveal to us the depth of our own souls. He alone can bring us peace. But we look for these things on his terms, not ours. We do not create or define our own salvation. God has defined it for us.

Jesus Christ has not come into the world to solve our problems or guarantee our happiness, to make our faith "work for us." He has come to satisfy our hunger for deeper, richer, more authentic life – what the Gospel calls "abundant life." He came so that we do not have to live as lonely, isolated selves adrift in a universe that makes no sense to us. In Jesus God has come to live with us in the midst of our humanity, with all our fear, confusion, sorrow and pain, and to give us a share in life eternal, the divine life. We come to this sanctuary each Sunday not to enlist God in service of our dreams of success and happiness, but to find our connection with God through Jesus Christ. And in doing that, we discover in deeper and deeper ways our connection with each other and with every other human being. That connection, by the way, is what helps so many Christians get through their hard times.

Belief in Jesus Christ does not make life any easier, but *he* makes it fuller and more meaningful. And for those in hard circumstances – which is all of us sooner or later -- he offers grounds for hope: hope that sadness will be turned into joy, mourning into dancing, and death into life. Our hope is not in ourselves and our belief, or in any earthly power, but in the One John has pointed us to.

We come here each Sunday to meet the One who comes to us again and again to let us know that we do not face the world alone. The true light, that enlightens everyone, is coming into the world.

Grace Presbyterian Church
Springfield, VA
December 14, 2014

Providential Mercy

God's mercy is revealed in God's abundant provision for the needs of God's people: manna in the wilderness, loaves and fish in Galilee, the "bread of life" in the person of Jesus Christ – miracles of mercy raining down from heaven.

A Meal Is Not Just about the Food
Matthew 14: 13-21

A few years ago, I heard a news item about a man who had conducted a human behavior experiment. The experiment involved going to restaurants and asking other diners, who were total strangers, for a taste of what was on their plates. Astoundingly, most people (about 75%) complied, willingly offering the man a mouthful of whatever they had ordered, often on their own forks. As he analyzed the results across restaurant visits, the man observed that the more high-end the restaurant, the greater the degree of compliance with his outlandish request. The news story didn't offer any theories as to why people eating in fancy restaurants were more willing to let a stranger eat from their plates, but I'll hazard a guess. The great food writer M.F.K. Fisher noted that sharing food is an act of intimacy: maybe these mostly well-off diners were looking for a taste of human community, so they were willing to give a well-dressed stranger a taste of their food. A meal is not just about the food – it can be a chance to make new friends.

I suspect such a phenomenon could be observed only in a wealthy society where there is a food culture, where food is not associated primarily with sustenance but with new taste experiences. The crowd Jesus fed with two fish and five loaves of bread would probably not have had the luxury of sharing their food with strangers that the well-off restaurant patrons did. It is likely that many of the people who gathered on the beach in Galilee that day were chronically hungry. Jesus had tried to be alone, going off in a boat to a "deserted place," but they followed him – they must have been walking along the shore, multitudes of them, keeping pace with the movement of his boat. No doubt some of them were hungry for his words about the kingdom of heaven, while others were just plain hungry. Whoever they were, they couldn't get enough of him, because they stayed and stayed, not even getting up to go home at dinnertime.

Jesus himself, at this point in the Gospel, is at a low point in his ministry. His fame is spreading, but so is opposition to him. He has been rejected in his hometown of Nazareth, and he has already tangled with the Pharisees more than once. Even worse, he has just received the news that John the Baptist has been beheaded, executed for the gruesome entertainment of the guests at a Roman banquet, and his head displayed on a platter. So, when Jesus tries to retreat from the crowds, he is exhausted and sick at heart. Yet he had compassion for that crowd: he healed the sick people among them and he fed them.

The feeding of the 5000 is the only miracle story found in all four Gospels, and Matthew essentially tells it twice. Clearly this story had a special place in the memory of the early church. Neither Matthew nor any of the other three evangelists give us the slightest clue as to how Jesus did this. All they really want us to know is that hungry people were fed and it was because of Jesus. And the miracle of the meal wasn't just about the food – the miracle was Jesus' presence among them, feeding the hunger of their souls along with the hunger of their bodies.

This meal on the shore of the Sea of Galilee was about so much more than the food. Jesus's presence there, and the miracle of God's provision revealed in him, brought back the memories of ancient Israel. The people would have remembered the stories of the manna in the wilderness, when they were refugees from Egypt, frightened and hungry, and God bent down to them and fed them. They would have remembered the story of Elisha, who took an offering of a few loaves and some ears of grain during a time of famine and fed it to a hundred hungry people. The Hebrew psalmists wrote poetry about God's miracles of provision: "Mortals ate the bread of angels: God sent them food in abundance…and they ate and were well-filled" (Ps. 78: 25-29). When people saw Jesus and his disciples passing out baskets and baskets of food, they remembered all the stories of God's abundance. This meal was about so much more than the food.

Shared food does create intimacy. Quite apart from the multiplication of the loaves, what happened between Jesus and the people on that faraway shore was just as surprising as what happened between the diners in the posh restaurant I described earlier. In the ancient world people did not share food casually. It was important to choose your dinner companions very carefully, because according to ancient custom, someone who came into your tent and shared your meal could no longer be your enemy. Sharing a meal bound you to a person. That's why the Pharisees got so upset when Jesus ate with tax collectors, prostitutes and other assorted sinners. He was declaring his acceptance of them, even his friendship with them. So, think of what was going on on that beach in Galilee: in providing this miraculous meal, Jesus was binding all these people to himself and, in the process, binding them to each other. This meal was not just about the food.

Many years ago, I heard a story about a boy who could not eat because of a congenital disorder – he had to receive his nutrition through a gastric tube. His parents had to fight the system to get him into school and camp, because they wanted to give him as normal a life as possible. Still, his life was not normal. When he went to camp, the hardest time for him was when all the children sat around the campfire and roasted marshmallows. On one of these occasions, a camp counselor asked him how he was feeling, and this is what he said: "I'm happy for them that they can enjoy that food. It must taste so good." His mom said what he was really saying is something like this: "It hurts that I can't be part of that – but I'm happy just to be around the campfire with them." Being part of that community was important enough to this little boy that he was willing to suffer pain for it. A meal is not just about the food.

There is a church in New York City that has been serving 1200 meals a day to the city's hungry people since 1982. The story of this church is something of a miracle itself. By the early 1980s, the church had experienced drastically declining membership and rising maintenance costs, and the Episcopal bishop of New York wanted to shut it down. But people kept coming to the church for help. The congregation thought that "if Holy Apostles was going out of business anyway, it might as well do some good before it did," so they opened a soup kitchen. The soup kitchen did well, and donations started coming in. The congregation was able to repair their leaking roof and ceiling, but when the work was almost done there was a fire. The firefighters had to break the church's beautiful, antique stained-glass windows to vent the gases from the fire; when it was all over the church stood "blackened, dripping, and open to the sky." Nevertheless, they served lunch to 950 people the next day, and have continued to serve daily meals ever since. The associate rector, who was interviewed for an article about the church, said this: "Those of us who worship at Holy Apostles feel we have a Sunday-Monday connection. The bread and wine of the Eucharist become the food we share with our neighbors during the week."[23] A meal is not just about the food.

A long time ago, Jesus stood before a crowd of people with all kinds of hunger: physical, emotional, spiritual. He lifted his hands, and blessed, broke and shared the food of God, a meal from heaven. He shared this meal with total strangers; he shared it with the poor and hungry; he shared it with the lost and the lonely, the sick and disabled; he shared it with sinners of all varieties; and here at this table, he shares this heavenly meal with you and me.

A meal is not just about the food.

Grace Presbyterian Church
Springfield, VA
August 3, 2014

---

[23]Ian Frazer, "Hungry Minds," *The New Yorker*, May 26, 2008, 56-65.

Inclusive Mercy

God's mercy is revealed in God's gracious inclusion of the outcast, the "other," and the ungodly. The promise of blessing under the covenant with God's people does not negate God's freedom to bestow blessing outside it. And when we get to the category of the "ungodly," we must include ourselves, who have been brought into the covenant by Jesus Christ, not according to what we deserve (or think we deserve) but according to his mercy.

Divine Economics
Genesis 21: 8-21

It could almost be a 21st-century situation: an aging couple, after years of trying unsuccessfully to have a child, finally takes matters into their own hands. They secure the services of a surrogate mother, and have a child at last. And then, lo and behold, the wife gets pregnant! Now there are two children, and the couple is doubly blessed.

I say it could *almost* be a contemporary situation; the situation of Abraham, Sarah, and their two sons is a little more complicated than that. Contemporary surrogate moms are not household slaves like Hagar, and they are not essentially second wives, as Hagar became to Abraham. Isaac's birth to Sarah and Abraham in their old age, fourteen years after Ishmael's birth, just exacerbated tensions that were already building up in this family. The situation in Abraham's household was headed toward meltdown.

How did this family get to such a point? Sarah's joy in bearing Isaac, the gift-child of God, the son of laughter, has hardened into mistrust and jealousy. What has tipped the balance in this delicate family situation?

Sarah probably had some lingering resentment over Hagar's condescension toward her after Ishmael was conceived. (You can read about that in chapter 16.) In Sarah's world women got status by having children; Hagar's quick success and Sarah's long failure in this department caused Hagar, even in her low-status position as a foreign slave, to look down on Sarah, and Sarah was intuitive enough to pick up those signals. And then of course there was the question of the legitimate heir. It wasn't about money as much as it was about the elect destiny of Abraham's heirs, election that included the promise of land and progeny. Sarah's anxiety over the possibility of the firstborn Ishmael usurping what was rightfully Isaac's went completely off the charts one day as she watched the two children playing together. Sarah decided it was time to take action. She ordered Abraham to tell Hagar and Ishmael to pack their bags.

However, Hagar and Ishmael are not so easily discarded. Abraham naturally does not want to see his son go (though he seems to care little enough about Hagar). It is only because God tells him to comply with Sarah's wishes that he gets up early the next day to send the mother and son into the wilderness with barely enough to keep them alive for a few days. This will not be the last time that Abraham is told to sacrifice a son; his later experience on Mount Moriah with Isaac has some haunting connections with Ishmael's banishment to the desert. (Isaac and Ishmael are re-united at Abraham's grave in chapter 25; it's interesting to speculate on the conversation they might have had about life with Dad.)

Hagar, of course, has done nothing to deserve Abraham and Sarah's ill-treatment of her and her son. The surrogate mom arrangement was certainly not her choice, and after being commandeered into the old couple's plan for begetting an heir, she is cast aside when her services are no longer needed. Sarah's anxiety over her own son's future leads her to act heartlessly toward Hagar and Ishmael. She deals with her anxiety by distancing herself from Hagar, emphasizing the outsider status of the woman who has shared her household: "Cast out this slave woman with her son."

Sarah's behavior, though cruel, is certainly not exceptional. It reflects a natural impulse of any of us when we feel threatened by someone from the outside who might undermine our place in the pecking order. Think of the threat American workers feel when immigrants begin taking jobs in key industries.

Behind all this anxiety and insecurity is the belief that life is a kind of zero-sum proposition. When I took economics in graduate school many years ago, a simple working definition of "the dismal science" that we used was "the study of how scarce resources are allocated." We graphed utility functions and preference functions, based on the premise that within resource constraints, a person maximizes a preference for one good at the expense of another, or a society allocates goods to one group of people at the expense of another group. If I gain something here, I must lose something somewhere else; or you must lose something as it is redistributed to me.

If this is the way the world works, then its goods and benefits need to be controlled and managed. Getting what we need or think we deserve becomes a matter of taking charge of our lives, as Abraham and Sarah did in arranging for the birth of Ishmael by co-opting Hagar's womb.

There is no doubt that these economic models tell us something about the way goods are allocated in a society. Societies do make choices, between guns and butter, prisons and schools, highways and libraries. Investing lots of resources in one area means investing fewer in another. If there's only a certain amount of good stuff to go around, somebody will benefit and somebody will suffer. No wonder we get anxious!

That is not how God looks at the world, though. Isaac and Ishmael are *both* children of promise. It's worth noting that both of them get genealogies in chapter 25; that's the Bible's way of saying that somebody is important, and clearly, Ishmael is important to God. At the point of death in the harsh Middle Eastern wilderness, the boy whose name means "God hears" is heard and helped. "Do not be afraid, Hagar – for God has heard the voice of the boy where he is. Lift him up and hold him fast with your hand, for I will make a great nation of him." And just as on Mount Moriah with Isaac, God provides: Hagar opens her eyes and there is a well brimming with water, and the lives of the mother and son are saved.

In making a covenant with Isaac, God had no intention of overlooking Ishmael. Ishmael will follow a different path to his destiny, but he will follow this path carrying the promises of God. God's blessing is more expansive than we usually like to imagine. The promise of blessing under the covenant doesn't negate God's freedom to bestow blessing outside of it. The Bible makes this point over and over again:

- A poor Moabite woman named Ruth becomes the ancestor of the great King David.

- A Syrian general called Naaman, the commander of an enemy army, is given the gift of miraculous healing.

- God sends the reluctant prophet Jonah to the Babylonian city of Nineveh to seek the repentance and salvation of the Ninevites.

- When the people of Israel are exiles in Babylon, God tells Jeremiah to seek the welfare of that hated foreign city.

What all this means is that the destiny of the people of Israel is intertwined with that of the people around it. When Jesus pointed out memorable instances of God's mercy toward outsiders to the people of Nazareth, he got run out of town (Lk 4:16-30); and his own acts of mercy toward foreigners, tax collectors, prostitutes and other sinners eventually helped him get crucified.

That's zero-sum thinking in action. If God loves these outsiders, God must love us less. If there's more blessing over there, there must be less blessing here. The sad fact of Christian mistreatment of the Jews over the centuries is in some sense a reflection of that mindset: the belief that in creating a brand-new people of God, the church, God must have turned away from the original covenant people, the Jews. And both rabbinic Judaism and Christian interpretation have sometimes used the story of Ishmael's threat to Isaac's inheritance to justify demonizing Ishmael's descendants, Muslim Arabs.

The purpose of a covenant people of God, whether we are talking about the covenant with Israel or the covenant in Jesus Christ, is not to be hoarders and gatekeepers of God's blessing. The sole purpose of the covenant people is to point out to other people the character and works of the God who created, sustains, and is redeeming the whole world. Our purpose is to point to the God whose blessing spills out even in places we wouldn't expect.

We are all recipients of immeasurable blessing. According to the Apostle Paul, we are all freed slaves who have received our deliverance from the tyranny of sin and death by the sheer grace of God. Any attempt to put boundaries on that gift of salvation, to treat it as a zero-sum proposition, means that we have not really received it as the gift of a free and sovereign and generous God.

Perhaps Sarah and Abraham's biggest failure was in forgetting the astonishing gift of Isaac's presence, turning the occasion of their miraculous parenthood into another occasion to control and possess. Having been delivered from the oppression of childlessness, brought by the grace of God into a future that is truly open and full of promise, they are not prevented from becoming oppressors themselves. They try to secure for their exclusive enjoyment a gift freely given.

The secret to living more generously, more compassionately with others is simply to remember what has been given to us. We all stand before God with nothing of our own – and the God who provides water in the desert and the promise of new life stands ready to pour blessings into our outstretched hands. In the wideness of God's mercy, there is enough for all.

Idylwood Presbyterian Church
Falls Church, VA
June 22, 2008

Going to the Dogs
Matthew 15: 21-28

Are there any dogs that have places of honor in your household? Do they get hugged and caressed? Do they enjoy lots of treats and privileges? If so, that is not surprising. In general, we love dogs in America. Dogs have had their own TV shows and movies. If we have them as pets we often let them sleep on our beds, we take them on vacation with us, and we mourn them when they die. The care, feeding, and happiness of dogs is a huge industry in the U.S. and in many other parts of the world as well.

It hasn't always been that way. In the ancient world, dogs were not held in such high esteem. In fact, they were considered a nuisance and a threat. The dogs of the ancient Mediterranean were not the Yorkies, Labradors, Airedales or other fetching breeds we fancy today. They weren't soft, shaggy, sleek, or cuddly. They were what you might call "mangy curs." You see these dogs today all over parts of Asia and North Africa, gaunt yellow creatures with hungry eyes. They live on the outskirts of cities and come into human population centers to scavenge for food. Sometimes people take pity on them and feed them, but mostly they are ignored or persecuted. Unlike the dogs of North America, they lead, it must be said, a dog's life.

In the ancient Jewish world, calling someone a dog was about the worst thing you could say to him. No one would say something like "You sly dog!" as a way of showing approval.

So it is hard to soften Jesus' words to the Canaanite woman. Lots of commentators have tried. Some have said the word he used was really something more like "doggie" or "poochie," but that doesn't change the harshness of what he said all that much. Others say Jesus was testing the woman to see if she had enough faith. Still others say that Jesus's words to the woman only seem harsh by our modern, politically correct standards.

None of this really works, though. No matter how we look at it, Jesus tried to turn away a request for help, and did so by calling a gentile woman a dog. We read this story, and we end up liking and admiring the woman and wondering about the Jesus we thought we knew.

Who was this woman? She was a Canaanite, which put her in the category of the ancient enemies of God, the idol-worshipers who had once occupied the Promised Land. She was a Gentile, which made contact with her something to be strenuously avoided. She was from the region of Tyre and Sidon, cities which were considered economic oppressors of Israel. And she was a woman, which put her on the fringes of things no matter where she was from.

This woman was seriously overstepping some boundaries when she approached Jesus. A lone woman simply did not approach a group of men, and especially not a religious leader like Jesus, and certainly not if she wasn't even Jewish. The disciples tell Jesus to get rid of the woman, which is what they are always telling him to do with inconvenient people. But in this case, even Jesus is unfriendly. At first, he tries to ignore her, and when she will not be ignored, he doesn't hesitate to put her in her place. "I was sent to the lost sheep of Israel," he says. *Not to the likes of you!* In other words, "if I start taking my ministry to the Gentile dogs, then the children of Israel will be cheated."

Maybe he was at the end of his rope with all the human need that was constantly brought before him wherever he went. People never left him alone. They were always following him around, wanting him to do something for them, but they didn't seem to recognize or care who he was. Well, this woman was getting ready to tell him who he was.

The woman is incredibly pushy. She will not take no for an answer. Desperate situations call for desperate measures, and the Canaanite woman recognizes Jesus as the only hope for her daughter.

The woman claims no rights for herself. She does not believe her needs or her daughters have any priority. But she's heard of this man, Jesus of Nazareth, who is known for taking on hard cases. So with no rights or relationship to claim, she makes an appeal to his mercy.

This woman is one of the most remarkable persons in all of the New Testament. She caused Jesus to change his mind! You could even say she won a theological argument with him by defining his mission in a new way. She turned an insult to her advantage, letting him know that in *her* household children and dogs *both* ate, and at the same time.[24] Jesus must have admired her wit and her courage, and he commended her for her faith.

By this point in Matthew's Gospel, Jesus has fed 5000 people with five loaves of bread and two fish. He has calmed a storm and healed an untold number of people of their diseases and disabilities. He has preached the Sermon on the Mount. He has told parables that have opened doors to the mystery of the kingdom of heaven. And now a nervy woman who isn't even Jewish has changed his mind? I should note that Jesus did not say anything to her that wasn't true. He *was* sent first to the lost children of Israel. That was always the plan. But it was only the first part of the plan, and this woman gave him the opportunity to see, in a flash, the whole scope of his mission in the world. This intrepid woman essentially defined for Jesus who he was: the merciful Savior of *all* people.

When you think about it, Jesus had already set people up to challenge the conventional wisdom about who would be included in God's kingdom. He has described the kingdom of God as a place where weeds are allowed to grow along with the valuable cash crop; a place where an invasive plant is encouraged to flourish in a well-cultivated garden; a place where a kind of yeasty ferment is constantly shaking things up (Matt. 13: 24-33). It's a messy kind of kingdom that Jesus describes. A kingdom like that would have to include some pushy Gentile women and other undesirables.

Matthew has given us an amazing story. It reminds me of another story, in Genesis (18: 22-23), when Abraham bargains with God to spare the inhabitants of Sodom. His argument is essentially this: "Yes, I know the people of this city are guilty of all kinds of evil. But what if you can find fifty righteous people in the city? Will you

---

[24]Judith Gundry-Volf, "Spirit, Mercy, and the Other," *Theology Today* 51:4 (January 1995), 518.

cause them to perish along with all the wicked ones?" "Far be it from you" – the Lord of heaven and earth – "to do such a thing!" Abraham says. God relents and promises to forgive them, and Abraham carries the argument forward, so that eventually God agrees not to condemn the city even if only a handful of righteous people can be found in it. Do you see what Abraham was doing? He was essentially reminding God of who God is – a God whose nature it is to be merciful. Abraham changed the terms of the argument by appealing to God's mercy.

I think that's what the Canaanite woman was doing, too. She was changing the terms of the argument. The Canaanite woman believed that God has mercy not only for the righteous and deserving and chosen ones, but for everyone. She believed that the boundaries for the mercy of God were not drawn between the region of the Galilee and that of Tyre and Sidon. She believed what Peter later said to people who wanted to keep the Gentiles out of the church: "God shows no partiality" (Acts 10:34).

There is an old prayer that the church used to say on Communion Sundays. It goes like this: "We do not presume to come to your table, merciful Lord, trusting in our own goodness, but in your all-embracing love and mercy. We are not worthy even to gather up the crumbs under your table, but it is your nature always to have mercy. So, feed us with the body and blood of Jesus Christ, your Son, that we may forever live in him and he in us."

Brothers and sisters in Christ, we are all Canaanite women. We stand before God not because we, the church of Jesus Christ, have some special privilege, and certainly not because we are so righteous, but simply because God has included us. God has included us because it is the nature of God to be merciful – and if God's Son needed to be reminded of that by a nameless Canaanite woman, so much the better for all of us. So, let us take these precious crumbs of all-embracing mercy and scatter them through the world.

Good Samaritan Presbyterian Church
Waldorf, MD
August 14, 2011

In the Shadow of the Cross
Matthew 21: 1-11, 27: 11: 54

I've had a long-standing grievance with Fairfax County Public Schools for scheduling spring break during Holy Week. That schedule means that many of our families are away during the church's remembrance of Jesus' last week on earth. It always makes me feel sad that there are so few of us here to go with him to the upper room and Gethsemane, Pilate's headquarters and the journey to the cross. Holy Week actually affords a great privilege for Christians: the opportunity to remain for a while in the shadow of the cross, hearing the story of a Lord who confuses and frightens the world and suffers for it, and whose suffering redeems the world. So that is what we are doing today, just for a while, and I pray that during this Holy Week you will find other occasions to seek the paradoxical peace of that shadow.

Jesus's last week on earth is framed by two public processions. The first one, the entry into Jerusalem, is joyful, while the second one is ghastly: the journey from Pilate's judgment hall to the cross on Calvary is a wretched affair of pain, insults and humiliation as the crowds turn out to watch the spectacle of a condemned man stumbling toward his execution. The hero who entered Jerusalem to shouts of "hosanna" the previous Sunday has become the victim of Friday.

The first procession was carefully staged by Jesus and scripted by the Hebrew Bible. First, he came down from the Mount of Olives, the place that Zechariah had said would be the staging ground for God to fight the enemies of Israel and restore Jerusalem to glory (14: 4). The donkey Jesus rode is also from Zechariah: the coming king would be a military hero, both triumphant and humble (9: 9-10). To many in the crowds streaming into Jerusalem for Passover, these symbols could mean only one thing: the king who was coming would put an end to the hated Roman oppression. As they spread their garments on the road in front of him, they were re-enacting a coronation custom from Old Testament times.

Some scholars say it was this procession that got Jesus arrested. They point to evidence of a ceremonial Roman procession going on the very day Jesus entered Jerusalem. The Roman parade would have been an intimidating display of imperial power, and would have sent a strong signal to anyone in the crowds gathering for Passover who might have been thinking about an uprising or even a protest. Jesus' outrageous counter-procession, a mockery of Roman pomp and power, would have been seen as a deliberate provocation, a brazen bit of street theater designed to draw crowds away from the imperial display.

The crowds, at any rate, may well have been confused by what was going on. Some people must have thought it was a joke, an occasion for merriment, like a Mardi Gras parade, while others saw the fulfillment of prophecy.

As the week wore on, it became clear that Jesus was not the conquering hero many people thought he was, and his tangles with the religious authorities began to mark him as a condemned man. Once it became clear that things were going to go south for him, people were ready to rethink their allegiance.

Their behavior should come as no surprise to us. Haven't we all observed that people like to hitch their wagons to a winner? Whenever there is an election, we see people shifting their allegiances late in the game, when they can see who looks most likely to win. People want to be seen supporting a winner, not a loser. When our heroes' fortunes begin to turn, we distance ourselves from them. It's not just politicians who say one thing one minute and another the next; it's human nature to be fickle in that way.

It is a tradition in some churches to have a dramatic reading of the Passion narrative on Palm Sunday, with the congregation taking the role of the crowd and shouting, "Let him be crucified!" Some church members have a hard time doing that. Why do you suppose that is? It is because most of us do not like to believe that we are the kind of people who could have been persuaded to turn against Jesus, to deny him, or judge him, or dismiss him. We all like to believe that if we had been among the disciples, we wouldn't have deserted him; that if we'd been in the crowd, we would have protested against releasing Barabbas instead of Jesus.

But what Matthew wants us to see is that these were ordinary people in Jerusalem. They were not bad people; for the most part, they were simply afraid and impressionable. The religious authorities were afraid of what the Romans would do to them if Jesus were really proclaimed as King of the Jews. Pilate was afraid of the crowds and the possibility of arrest escalating to full-scale violence. The disciples were afraid of being seen associating with a marked man. Matthew is telling us that given the right circumstances, we are all capable of inconstancy, cowardice, faithlessness, and cooperation with evil.

When we become Christian, we're supposed to give up our pretenses of innocence. Yet like Pilate washing his hands, we seem to have a desperate need to believe we are innocent. The news media give us a daily stream of stories of corruption, cheating, and general mayhem; though we may feel distressed at the general lawlessness of the world, it is hard to deny the feelings of moral superiority these stories may afford us. We watch the antics of public figures trying to cover their tracks and say to ourselves, with relief, "I'm not like that."

But here is the offensive part of the Christian gospel, the part we have a hard time wrapping our minds around: Jesus, in going to his shameful, excruciating death outside the gates of Jerusalem, did not make a distinction between the bandits on the other two crosses and the upright, law-abiding religious people. He did not make a distinction between the cowardly, self-serving Pilate and his own frightened disciples. He does not make a distinction between the Wall Street bankers who brought down the economy and the people they victimized. He does not make distinctions. He died for all.

This message was just as offensive in New Testament times as it is now. The apostles had to struggle with what it meant to include Gentiles in the first Christian communities. Gentiles were the "ungodly." Gentiles worshiped idols. They were sexually immoral. They were greedy. They were sinful. But here they were, discovering that Christ had died for them, too. Paul said, "there is no distinction, because *all* have sinned and fall short of the glory of God" (Rom. 3:23).

That's what the tearing of the temple curtain is all about. Matthew is letting us know that in Jesus' death the dividing line between two classes of humanity has been breached – even the godless and the lawless are not out of the reach of God's love in Jesus Christ. Jesus has loved all of us enough to set aside the very thing that set him apart from us, his sinlessness, and to die the degrading death of a criminal.

This, by the way, is why Christians are supposed to pray for their enemies. We pray for them because they are also people for whom Christ died. We are supposed to try to see our enemies from the perspective of Jesus on the cross, looking down at the soldiers who were casting lots for his clothing, at the crowd of people who spit on him and mocked him, at the passersby who simply turned away with indifference – all of them the very people he was dying for. He died not only for his friends, but also for his enemies.

I am very glad of that, because I can't rely on the constancy of my own friendship. I can only rely on a Lord who has demonstrated, to the fullest extent possible, his love for both our best and our worst selves.

In that knowledge we all may find, even in the shadow of the cross that lengthens and darkens as we go through this Holy Week, comfort and assurance and gratitude.

Grace Presbyterian Church
Springfield, VA
April 13, 2014

The View from the Ditch
Luke 10:25-37

On San Francisco's Ocean Beach, there used to be a tourist attraction called a *camera obscura*. It was simply a small chamber fitted with a large moving lens; you enter the chamber and look through the lens, and as you do, the familiar contours of the world you know begin to shift. Familiar sights – the beach, the gulls, the blue line of the ocean – suddenly look unfamiliar and mysteriously more beautiful. Just as you begin to get used to one view of the seascape, it changes, so that you're left feeling a bit disoriented and, according to one writer, freshly entranced.[25]

Perhaps we need something like a *camera obscura* to give us a fresh look at Luke's oh-so-familiar story of the "Good Samaritan." This story Jesus told in response to a challenge from a lawyer is one of the best known in all of Scripture. The label "Good Samaritan" has become a cliché for any kind-hearted person who goes out of his way to help someone in need.

The Samaritan is not the main character of the story, though. The story is framed by a debate between Jesus and a lawyer, not a member of the bar but a religious scholar, versed in the law of Moses. "A lawyer stood up to test Jesus." Already we know his intentions are not entirely sincere. He is not looking to learn anything, he's looking to be reinforced in his own good opinion of himself.

And the debate, it turns out, revolves around the definition of the term "neighbor." The lawyer begins by asking Jesus about the prerequisites for eternal life, and Jesus bounces the question back to him: "What is written in the law?" When the lawyer gives the right answer – "You shall love the Lord your God with all your heart, and soul, and mind, and strength, and your neighbor as yourself" – Jesus commends him for his spot-on answer. "Right," he says. "Now just do it." The lawyer has something else up his

---

[25] William T. Vollman, "Upside Down and Backward," *The Best American Essays 2001*, ed. Kathleen Norris (Boston/New York: Houghton Mifflin, 2001), 296-297.

sleeve, though. "Who," he asks, perhaps with a crafty smile playing around his lips, "is my neighbor?"

The man's question, though motivated by self-interest, was a legitimate one. Scripture did not speak entirely with one voice on this matter. According to Leviticus 19:18, a "neighbor" is a member of the children of Israel; but then, later in the chapter, a "neighbor" also becomes a stranger or foreigner, whom the Israelites are to treat as a citizen and love as themselves.

There had to be some limits, though, the lawyer must have been thinking. His real question was, "Who is *not* my neighbor?" *What is my margin of error on this? Whom can I afford to snub or slight or even legitimately hate?* The subtext of this question, of course, is "How can I be expected to treat *everybody* as a neighbor? There are limits on my time, resources, and good will."

Surely that is a question you have asked, too. It's a question that comes up far more often than we would like. I may be happy to give money to a relative who needs something to tide him over until he starts working again, but does that mean I am supposed to open my pockets to every vagrant or bag lady who has their hand out? Surely not.

Who is my neighbor? Who is not my neighbor? Let us define some limits. The question is offered for debate, but Jesus is not interested in quibbling over the fine points of scriptural interpretation. What he's interested in is clarifying the essence of neighborliness, and he does so by telling a story about something that happened on the Jericho Road. It is a story that would have profoundly disoriented everyone who heard it.

There is a scene in Tom Wolfe's *Bonfire of the Vanities* in which the main character, Sherman, and his girlfriend, Maria, take the wrong exit off the freeway and find themselves, in Sherman's Mercedes, in the Bronx. It is a moment of sheer panic for them, because they know they are in a place they have no business being. The Jericho Road in New Testament times and even today, I'm told, would arouse the same fear that the South Bronx did for Wolfe's characters. The road from Jerusalem to Jericho is only sixteen miles long, but it descends over 3600 feet in that short distance. It is a steep, rough, treacherous road, where roving bands of highwaymen went in search of victims. The general wisdom was that you would have to be crazy to travel that road alone and unarmed. We don't know the circumstances of the man in Jesus' story, only that he was one of the victims of the frequent muggings on the Jericho Road.

The man is just a man, nameless, faceless, beat-up, lying in a ditch. The story revolves around the other travelers on the road who see him lying there. The first two, a priest and a Levite, go out of their way to avoid the man. We don't know exactly why they didn't stop. Maybe they just assumed somebody else would. Maybe they were afraid of disqualifying themselves from their religious duties; any contact with a dead body would make them ritually impure, and the body in the ditch probably looked dead. So maybe they were just being conscientious about their work, making sure they were fit to do their important jobs in the Temple. The way Jesus was telling the story, his audience would have been expecting the third person to come along, the one who would finally rescue the man, to be an ordinary Israelite.[26] But Jesus shocked everyone by telling them that the person who came to the man's rescue was a Samaritan.

Samaritans were considered to be enemies of Israel. They were "descendants of a mixed population" that had occupied the land ever since the conquest by Assyria centuries earlier.[27] They had their own place of worship away from the Jerusalem temple. They were social outcasts, ceremonially unclean, and heretical. They were not considered to be the people of God. To hear a story about a "good" Samaritan, a merciful, compassionate person who took care of the mugging victim at considerable trouble and expense to himself, was just not what anyone expected.

No one could have been more disoriented by the story than the lawyer himself. Jesus had not answered his question, but had turned it completely around. The lawyer's question was, *To whom do*

---

[26] David Buttrick, *Speaking Parables: A Homiletic Guide* (Louisville: Westminster John Knox, 2000), 184.

[27] Fred B. Craddock, *Luke* (Louisville: John Knox Press, 1990), 150.

I owe my concern? Who do I legitimately consider to inhabit my moral universe? Jesus' answer was, *Look who showed himself to be a neighbor to the man in the ditch – not at all whom you would expect.* And how did that Samaritan make the calculation of whether the man in the ditch deserved his attention? Apparently, not on the basis of anything he knew about the man. The man in the ditch has no distinguishing characteristics – remember, his assailants have stripped him and robbed him. He is unidentified by ethnicity, religion or social class. He *could* have been a Samaritan, but it's more likely that he was a Jew. He could have been a rich man or a poor man, a good citizen or a member of a highway gang himself. How did the Samaritan make the calculation?

The man in the ditch could be anyone. He could be a Christian or a Muslim or a Hindu. He could be your next-door neighbor or the guy whose daughter plays softball with your daughter. "He" could be the soccer mom down the street or the shopping-bag lady whose eyes you avoid at the supermarket. He could be a fellow church member or the scruffy-looking man with the sign on the exit ramp to the interstate. How will we make the calculation?

The man in the ditch could be anyone. He could be you yourself.

If the man in the ditch could be anyone, does the lawyer's question sound any different? If I am the man in the ditch, I am not going to care who it is that comes along to help me.

Many years ago, my husband and I were vacationing in Nova Scotia. We had scouted out a wooded hiking trail, and as the sun was going down we made our way back to our car. We arrived at our car only to find out that we had inadvertently locked the keys inside. We were dithering around trying to figure out what to do while the air grew colder and the light dimmer, when three men emerged from the woods and noted our distress. They were big, burly and unshaven; one of them was missing a tooth or two. The music from "Deliverance" started playing in our heads. The men offered us a ride to town in their pickup so that we could find a locksmith. As we climbed into the cab of the truck, we noticed the pile of guns in the back. It was a very uneasy ride to town for us, but the men were as good as their word and helped us all the way through our predicament, and would accept no payment for their trouble. We felt very ashamed for having doubted them, and were grateful beyond words for their kindness. Beyond all expectations, they had showed themselves to be neighbors to us.

Isn't it only right and natural to do for others what we would like to have done for us? When you put it that way, any talk of limits on our neighborliness begins to sound kind of lame. Who are we to decide who may inhabit our moral universe, and who may not?
After all, we worship a Savior who put no limits on his compassion. He is the One who spotted us from way down the road, saw us lying in the ditch, lost, abandoned, all but dead in our own lovelessness, and stopped to bathe and bandage and heal our wounds with the offering of his own life.

Turning the lens around so that we have the view from the ditch disorients us in order to reorient us. "Who is my neighbor?" is the wrong question. "How will you be neighborly?" is the question Jesus is asking us. "Where will you fit into someone else's view from the ditch?" It may be the most basic question of our lives.

Grace Presbyterian Church
Springfield, VA
June 26, 2016

Etiquette for the Kingdom of God
Luke 14: 1, 7-14

I don't know how the party Jesus attended at the Pharisee's house turned out, but it certainly got off to a rocky start. Luke's description almost makes me glad I wasn't there.

Before people even began to sit down for the meal, there was already tension in the air. The Pharisees were "watching Jesus closely," Luke tells us, suggesting that Jesus had been invited not because they wanted his company, but because they wanted to keep him in their sights. And Jesus did nothing to disarm them; in the part of our text that the lectionary leaves out, we learn that he provoked them by performing a Sabbath-day healing and then daring them to criticize him for it.

Continuing this display of bad manners as the dinner begins, he rebukes the guests for sitting down in the places of honor, and then turns his attention to his host, taking him to task for the composition of the guest list. I can't help thinking of that old jingle, "Every party needs a pooper, that's why we invited you."

Jesus's behavior was strange, when you think about it, because by all accounts, he loved parties. The Gospels tell us that he generally had so much fun at parties that he was accused by some of being a glutton and a drunk. But he doesn't seem to have been having much fun at this one. For that matter, I can't imagine the guests were having much fun, either. I think I'd need a dose of Paxil to enter that banquet hall. Even *before* Jesus entered the scene, there had to be a lot of anxiety in that room.

Meals in the ancient world were elaborate social ceremonies. No less than a high-profile Washington dinner party, they were occasions for the display of wealth and social power. Pliny the Younger provides a telling anecdote from the first century:

> Some very elegant dishes were served up to [my host] and a few more of the company; while those which were placed before the rest were cheap and

> paltry. He had apportioned in small flagons three different sorts of wine; but you are not to suppose it was that the guests might take their choice: on the contrary, that they might not choose at all. One was for himself and me; the next for his friends of lower order (for you must know that he measures out his friendship according to the degrees of quality); and the third was for his own freed-men and mine.[28]

In the rigidly stratified social world of the first century, dinner and luncheon parties were occasions where rank and status were clearly delineated; not to be aware of the boundaries was social suicide. So, when Jesus gave the guests advice about avoiding the places of honor at a dinner party, he seemed to be simply offering common-sense advice about how to avoid being embarrassed.

However, Jesus's intention seems to have been more subversive. Because when he turned to the host, what he had to say upset all the conventional ideas about entertaining at home.

Imagine being a prominent Washington host or hostess and being told something like this: "Stop inviting all the wealthy, good-looking, famous and powerful people to your parties. They are the ones who can return the favor by inviting you to *their* fabulous parties, where there will be lots of interesting conversation, insider tips about Washington politics, beautiful surroundings, and excellent food and wine. You don't want any of that stuff. What you should do is go out and invite some homeless people and social misfits. They will be poorly dressed, they'll eat up all your food and guzzle your wine without appreciating its quality, and they won't have anything interesting to talk about. They won't know anyone you'd like to be introduced to, and they'll drive away your more genteel friends. Can you start making the guest list now, please?"

---

[28] Pliny, the Younger *Letters* 2.6, in *Pliny: Letters*, trans. William Melmoth; rev. W.M.L. Hutchinson, LCL (Cambridge, Mass.: Harvard University Press, 1915), 109-11. Quoted by R. Allen Culpepper, "The Gospel of Luke," *New Interpreter's Bible, Volume IX* (Nashville: Abingdon Press, 1995), 286.

If Jesus came across as a poor sport at the Pharisee's house, it's because what he was witnessing there didn't seem to be a party at all, not by the standards of the kingdom of God. For Jesus, the way people acted at a party, both host and guests, was an indicator of how they understood the world. Social behavior was a sign of character. So, a party where people were stepping all over each other to get to the best seats and the host invited only the people who could offer him a return on his investment was not a real party. The problem with the folks at the Pharisee's house was not a problem of etiquette, it was the basic outlook of the host and his guests. The etiquette guide for losers Jesus seemed to be offering was actually a hospitality guide for the kingdom of God.

From a biblical perspective, a party is supposed to be a gospel celebration, a sign of God's kingdom breaking in, offering hope to the poor and oppressed, the least and the lost. A party is the Bible's symbol for God's hospitality. Listen to Isaiah's description of the great messianic banquet, where God will be the host: "…the LORD will make for all people a feast of rich food, a feast of well-aged wines…and wipe away the tears from all faces" (25: 6,8).

Notice that Isaiah says "all people." That is part of what Jesus was getting at when he told his host he should invite the poor and the lame and the blind – not the social elite, but the ones who have nothing of their own to bring. They can't offer anything in return for their invitation. One thing you can be sure of, they won't be heading for the "highest," most prestigious seats. They'll hang shyly by the door, afraid to take *any* seat, until the host comes over, puts a reassuring arm around their shoulders, pilots them to a table, and then introduces them to the other guests. That's what a party is like in the kingdom of God.

No wonder the Pharisees – who were the good Presbyterians of their day – were offended by Jesus's suggestions. He was turning upside down all the formulas that normal people lived by. If you had a place of honor at a banquet, it was because you had earned it, or your parents or grandparents had earned it for you. The formula is essentially the same today: get the right education, use the right language, wear the right clothes, go to the right church, and you will be hired by the best companies, be able to buy a house in the best neighborhoods, and have a place at the table at the best parties. If you are one of the insiders, this formula seems right and appropriate, and you are not going to appreciate anyone who challenges it.

Look at it another way, though: Jesus was offering a radical cure for anxiety – social, professional, and spiritual. By calling into question all systems of human merit or entitlement, Jesus cut to the heart of all of the ways in which people worry about whether they will measure up.

Of course, if you are one of those people who always get the place of honor, who feels secure in your place in the world, this may not sound like such good news. What is the fun of having premium-quality food and wine in a desirable location if everyone else is enjoying exactly the same things? Maybe the fun is to be able to relax and stop worrying about holding your place at the top of the pecking order, constantly scanning the room to see who might displace you. Maybe the fun is in the freedom toward yourself and other people that is suddenly open to you.

Jesus was always getting in trouble because he actually seemed to prefer the company of the people everyone else looked down on. Maybe it was because they were the only ones who weren't always trying to put themselves forward. They weren't so full of themselves that they couldn't see something in Jesus of Nazareth that they knew they didn't have. Maybe it was because they had such an acute sense of their own insufficiency, and were able to see in him something that they needed. Maybe that's what Jesus meant by saying that those who humble themselves will be exalted. The needy, vulnerable people that Jesus sought out were not worrying about how they measured up, because they knew they didn't. That gave them a kind of freedom that the socially and religiously well-placed people didn't have.

It is sometimes hard for us 21st century Presbyterians to hear this gospel word that Jesus speaks to us. For the most part, we are the social and religious insiders. We're not the ones hanging anxiously by the door or looking into the windows from outside. We have a voice in our social, civil and church communities.

Even so, we are no strangers to the fear of not measuring up. We are acutely conscious of things like degrees, titles, markers of professional accomplishment. We fret about what kind of schools our children will get into. We worry about staying in the middle or upper-middle class. Jesus the Lord addresses us amid our struggles to fit in or stay in, to make something of our lives, to believe that we have succeeded. He does not "measure out his friendship according to [our] degrees of quality" like that first-century host, but according to his infinite mercy.

That great party the Bible talks about -- not the one at the Pharisee's house, where the guests jockeyed for position -- but the great salvation feast, in which God wipes away the tears from all faces: that's the one we are invited to. It's for every one of us who has the sense to realize that we come bringing nothing of our own, and that if we are determined to stand on our own merits, we have already cut ourselves out of the picture. Our salvation is not in what we can achieve for ourselves, but in God's movement of grace toward us.

We have received an invitation we can never reciprocate. Jesus stands waiting as our host, ready to put reassuring arms around our shoulders and guide us to places of honor in the kingdom of God.

Grace Presbyterian Church
Springfield, VA
August 28, 2016

The Merciful Judge

The New Testament has varied metaphors for what God has done for humanity through the death and resurrection of Jesus: legal, financial, military, sacrificial. The forensic language of "justification" is especially pronounced in the Pauline letters. Paul uses this juridical metaphor as a way of talking about God's decision in our favor, "imputing" to us the righteousness of Christ. This is not a mechanical substitution, but God acting in Christ to put right what is wrong; since we do not have it in ourselves to repair our relationship with God, God has repaired it for us. God's saving love is not conditioned by our virtue, consistent good behavior, or even our belief; God acts toward us in a manner consistent with God's own loving and merciful nature, revealed in the death of Jesus. We need not fear condemnation because the Judge is also our Redeemer.

Relentless Mercy
Matthew 18:21-35

The problem Peter brings to Jesus is as old as humanity: "How many times must I forgive my brother (or sister)?" Peter is clearly wrestling with something big here, not the ordinary grievances and annoyances that are part of daily life both in and outside the church. How do you deal with the person who has really offended you, has done so over and over again, and doesn't seem to care? Are you supposed to just say, "Oh, that's OK" and move on, pretend it never happened? "How many times am I supposed to forgive?" says Peter, perhaps plaintively, "SEVEN times???"

Jesus's answer, which he gave in two parts, was probably not at all what Peter was hoping to hear. The first part of the answer sounds almost flip: not seven times, but seventy-seven times[29] – in other words, without limit. Jesus was probably playing on a story from Genesis, the story of Lamech (4:24). Lamech had no intention of forgiving his enemies, so he boasted that he would avenge himself not once, not twice, but seventy-seven times on anyone who dared to attack him. "Be the opposite of Lamech," Jesus says. "Let your forgiveness be as unrelenting as Lamech's revenge."

The second part of Jesus' response is in the form of a parable. Jesus takes a human problem and tells an exaggerated tale to help Peter to see it from a divine perspective. The parable involves two debtors and two creditors, but only three main characters. The central character is the debtor in the first part of the parable, the creditor in the second, and his problem is that he learns nothing from experience. In scene one of the drama, this servant, or agent, of the king has apparently embezzled a vast sum of money, and the day of reckoning has come. This "servant," or "slave" – it's the same word in Greek – is brought before the king to settle accounts. He owes the king an astounding amount of money – "ten thousand talents" would today be somewhere in the billions of dollars. The servant's request for some time to pay back the debt is desperate

---

[29] NRSV translation. The more familiar formula is "seventy times seven."

and pathetic – he will never be able to pay it back. He knows that his only real hope is to appeal to the king's mercy, and amazingly, the king responds. He is moved by pity, we are told, and he orders that the servant be released and forgives him the entire debt. Who can say why? He is the king, and he is free to forgive whom he will. He is free to bestow crushing punishments and astonishing gifts, and he chooses to bestow an astonishing gift.

In scene two of the parable, the former debtor becomes a creditor. Another servant of the king owes *him* money, a much smaller amount, say a thousand dollars. You would think that the guy who has been forgiven the billion-dollar debt would say, "Oh, why don't we just forget about this?" But he doesn't. Amazingly, he holds the other man accountable. The man's appeal for mercy is rejected, and he is thrown into debtors' prison, which is where the first man should have been.

Scene three: Some other servants of the king witness the first man's treatment of his debtor and are outraged. They report him to the king, who demands to see him. The king castigates the servant for his lack of mercy, especially in view of the mercy he has received, and hands him over to be tortured until he can pay the debt – which, of course, will be never.

All in all, it is not a pretty story. The first thing to remember is that it is a parable, not a strict allegory, and we are not to make a point-by-point connection between the king and God. But the terrible last words of the parable, suggesting there will be no mercy for the unmerciful, seems to be a comment on Peter's original question, "How many times do I have to forgive?" In other words, "how do I keep my own ledger books straight on this matter? I'm willing to forgive, but not too much, only what is reasonable and appropriate. After all, people do need to be held accountable."

Last week, the "Outlook" section of *The Washington Post* carried an essay about the case of Susan LeFevre, a wife and mother who sold drugs to an undercover police officer in Saginaw, Michigan in

1974.[30] She was nineteen years old at the time, and a first-time offender. She was sentenced to ten to twenty years in prison. One year into her prison term, she scaled a fence and escaped. She made her way to California, where she found work, eventually married, and has had three children. She volunteers for charitable causes, and has never committed another offense. Last year, thirty-two years after her escape, she was arrested and extradited to Michigan. Her lawyers have asked the judge to set aside the original drug sentence, but the district attorney has filed charges against her for escaping prison – if convicted, she could be sentenced to an additional five years on top of the original drug sentence.

The essay writer, Carol Steiker, a Harvard Law School professor, describes a new climate in our criminal justice system, a system now characterized by the "decline of mercy." Reformers have increasingly succeeded in limiting the power of judges, police departments, and juries to temper justice with mercy. Sentencing guidelines and mandatory minimum sentences have resulted in long prison terms for low-level, nonviolent offenders such as petty thieves and persons caught with small amounts of drugs. The result is a U.S. prison population of 2.3 million. In fact, the U.S. is the "world's leading incarcerator," locking up a greater number of offenders for longer periods of time than any other nation.[31] We are a prison state.

Now, I want to be clear: I am not suggesting that Jesus' command to his followers to "forgive seventy-seven times" means that the state should abandon its responsibility to protect its citizens from

---

[30] Carol S. Steiker, "Passing the Buck on Mercy," *The Washington Post*, September 7, 2008, B7.

[31] As of May 2017, there have been bipartisan efforts in Congress to roll back some of the most punitive sentencing guidelines and requirements for low-level offenders. Recent evidence suggests that "the age of incarceration is abating." (Charles Lane, "The decline of mass incarceration," *The Washington Post*, April 20, 2017, A19). However, the U.S. Attorney General has recently directed federal prosecutors to "pursue the most severe penalties possible, including mandatory minimum sentences, in his first step toward a return to the war on drugs of the 1980s and 1990s that resulted in long sentences for many minority defendants and packed U.S. prisons." (Sari Horwitz and Matt Zapotsky, "Sessions is resurrecting tough charging policies," *The Washington Post*, May 13, 2017, A1).

dangerous criminals. But I think it is worth asking, in this prison culture in which we live, what is the *purpose* of disciplinary action against an individual?

In Matthew's Gospel, right before today's lesson and as a lead-up to Peter's question, Jesus has some very unsentimental language about dealing with offenders in the church: First you point out the fault to the offender; if he doesn't listen to you, take along two others as witnesses, and if he still refuses to listen, tell it to the whole church. If the offender refuses to listen even to the church, only then is he shut out of the church's fellowship. Even then, the objective is to bring about repentance and welcome him back into the fellowship.

This approach has become the model for disciplinary action in the church. Its purpose is not punishment but restoration of the offender to the community. I'm not suggesting that the church's approach would work with criminal offenders, but the objective of restoration is worth considering. In the case of Susan Le Fevre, for example, what would be the purpose of putting her back in prison? She was told in 1974 to "turn her life around," and she has done that. The only purpose of her incarceration would be punishment. Perhaps justice will be served by refusing to commute the sentence, but assuredly mercy will not be done. I can't help wondering what it would mean to us as a society to make mercy an active principle in decisions about how to deal with both criminal and civil offenses. As well as being a prison state, we are also a highly litigious society, in which law-abiding citizens are forever hauling each other into court.

Maybe you are thinking that these reflections on our punitive culture are a long way from Peter's concern and Jesus' response. After all, most of us are concerned about how to forgive those who have hurt us personally – deeply, intentionally, and possibly repeatedly. Popular psychology tells us that we need to forgive for therapeutic reasons, in order to free ourselves from the crippling weight of our anger and resentment. That is true, of course, but that is not the point Jesus is making. Jesus wants to make a point about mercy.

John Calvin has suggested that our theology can help us here. "Assuredly," he writes, "there is but one way to achieve what is not merely difficult but utterly against human nature: to love those who hate us, to repay their evil deeds with benefits, to return blessings for reproaches. It is that we remember not to consider men's evil intentions but to look upon the image of God in them, which cancels and effaces their transgressions, and with its beauty and dignity allures us to love and embrace them."[32]

Was Calvin impossibly naïve? I don't think so – he recognized that in ourselves we have little power to forgive. Forgiveness, in the end, is a divine action, an operation of grace. It begins with the God who has forgiven us a debt we could never repay, who has wiped the slate clean and, through Christ, restored the image of God in us. As Paul says[33] in Colossians, "…when you were dead in your trespasses God made you alive together with [Christ], when he forgave us all our trespasses, erasing the record that stood against us with its legal demands. He set it aside, nailing it to the cross" (2:13-14).

Brothers and sisters in Christ, where our God is concerned, there will be no languishing in debtors' prison, no extradition to another state for our past crimes against the divine mercy, no building of a case against us. We have escaped the district attorney. We have been forgiven and restored, and what is asked of us is to remember, in our dealings with those who offend against us, the mercy that we have received.

It is not reasonable to ask the state to act with God's endless compassion, only to use the power it has to apply a principle of mercy. And it is perhaps not realistic for us to expect of ourselves the instant capacity to forgive seventy-seven times. But we are asked to submit all our grievances and demands for justice to the unrelenting mercy of God, asking for a power that may be beyond

---

[32] *Institutes of the Christian Religion,* ed. John T. McNeill, trans. Ford Lewis Battles, Vol. XX, III.vii.6 (Philadelphia: The Westminster Press, 1960), 697.

[33] Or someone writing in the Pauline tradition. Colossians is not among the undisputed seven letters written by Paul himself.

us, the power to forgive what seems unforgivable. We have to do, after all, with a God who raises from the dead – a God for whom nothing will be impossible.

Idylwood Presbyterian Church
Falls Church, VA
September 14, 2008

Credited with Righteousness
Genesis 15: 1-7, Romans 4: 13-25

On the day that former Virginia governor Bob McDonnell was found guilty of eleven counts of public corruption, a reporter covering the story talked with a maintenance worker named Kevin McGowan at the state Capitol building, just a few blocks away from the courthouse where the verdict was rendered. McGowan was surprised by the verdict, but not, he said, under any illusion "that any of the state's leaders lived up to their squeaky-clean images." In fact, he said, "Who's to say Thomas Jefferson was always on the up and up?"[34]

As we now know, Thomas Jefferson was not always "on the up and up." The man who wrote the Declaration of Independence was himself a slaveowner. He also initiated the removal of Indian tribes from their territory to make way for white settlers. In his political dealings he could be disloyal and opportunistic. In other words, this Founding Father of our nation was a human being, immensely talented and brave, but with his own faults and failings and hypocrisies.

Abraham, the founding father of our biblical faith, was also less than perfect. We first meet him in Genesis 12, when he is already 75 years old and God speaks to him and makes a staggering promise to him: that he will be the father of a great nation, with descendants more numerous than the stars. In order for this promise to be realized, Abraham and his wife, Sarai (later known as Sarah), will have to leave their home country and travel to an unknown place of God's choosing, with nothing but God's word to go on. By the time God speaks to Abraham again, at the beginning of chapter 15, many years have passed and Abraham, though still childless, has grown in wealth and stature and has become a worshiper of God. He has also resorted to some pretty shabby dealings to advance himself in the world. When he and Sarah go down to Egypt (12: 10-20), Abraham passes off his

---

[34] Laura Vozzella, "I think Jefferson would be appalled...it's so Illinois," *The Washington Post*, September 5, 2014, A6.

beautiful wife as his sister to protect himself from the murderous envy of the Egyptian men – as a consequence, she is taken into Pharaoh's house as a concubine. Pharaoh is so grateful to Abraham for this gift that he showers him with slaves and livestock. So, Abraham advances himself by throwing his wife under the bus. Even old Father Abraham himself wasn't always "on the up and up."

People are often shocked to read this lesser-known story about the first Patriarch, but Abraham's combination of fear and cunning is not exceptional among the biblical figures through whom God does great things. Jacob, for example, was a trickster and a cheat, David an adulterer who got his paramour's husband killed so he wouldn't find out who the real father of his wife's baby was.

In other words, Abraham, like these men, was an ordinary, flawed human being. In fact, Abraham might have been considered even less than ordinary, a virtual nonentity from an obscure village, who did not even have the distinction of fathering a child. It is not until God gets hold of this couple that they do anything to leave a mark on the world. As Eugene Peterson says in his paraphrase of Romans 4, "We call Abraham 'father' not because he got God's attention by living like a saint, but because God made something out of Abraham when he was a nobody."[35]

That is why Paul chooses Abraham's story to make a point about faith in Romans 4. "Abraham believed the Lord, and the Lord reckoned it to him as righteousness," we read in Genesis 15. As far as we can tell, God's word came to Abraham before he had any *belief* about God. Abraham didn't belong to a church or a temple, he had no Scriptures to read, nobody had passed on to him a body of doctrine about the existence of a singular deity who had the power to change a human life. Abraham and Sarah were tribal, tent-dwelling people, tied to the customs and beliefs of their ancestors. When Paul says that "God brings into existence the things that do not exist," I think it is fair to say that God also brought into existence Abraham's faith.

---

[35] *THE MESSAGE: The Bible in Contemporary Language* (NavPress Publishing Group, 2002).

Paul's point in Romans 4 is that Abraham's story is primarily a story about God, only secondarily a story about Abraham. Abraham had done nothing in particular to recommend himself to God, but God stooped down to him and his wife, creating literally out of nothing a new reality for this childless old couple. It would be decades before the promise was fulfilled and Isaac was born, but "Abraham believed God, and God reckoned it to him as righteousness."

The word "reckoned" has an archaic ring to it – we don't use it much anymore, except in certain parts of the country, where it is used to mean just "think" or "conjecture," as in "I reckon it will rain today." "Reckon" is actually an accounting term, which means "count" or, more to our purposes, "credit." "Abraham believed God, and God credited him with righteousness." God put something in the credit column of the ledger sheet for Abraham. It doesn't mean that God actually considered Abraham to be a righteous, virtuous man or that Abraham had already proved himself as such. It means that God planned in Abraham's favor based solely on Abraham's trust in God's good intentions toward him.

From a human point of view, Abraham and Sarah had nothing still to hope for. In a culture in which there was no concept of an afterlife, the only way you could live on was through your offspring, your heirs -- but Abraham and Sarah had lost that opportunity a long time ago. From a human point of view, their case was hopeless. When Paul says Abraham "hoped against hope," he means that he hoped against what is humanly reasonable to hope for. He hoped in spite of the evidence.

Paul tells the story of Abraham to the Roman Christians to remind them that whoever they are, whatever their origins -- Jewish or Gentile, model citizens or people with shady pasts and unsavory connections -- Abraham is their spiritual father, not by genetic inheritance but by faith. Anyone who believes in God's power and mercy in raising Jesus Christ from the dead for the redemption of the world is a descendant of Abraham and a child of God, an heir or heiress of all God's promises. Just as Abraham's faith was credited to him as righteousness, regardless of what he had been or done, so, Paul says, God will credit our faith, too. That is the radical message of the letter to the Romans.

My younger son and I enjoy the TV show "Mad Men," about the competitive world of the New York advertising industry in the 1960s. We were once talking about the latest episode in the company of some other people. Someone in the group said she had watched a few episodes of the show, but couldn't get involved in it because "all the characters are so despicable." I considered this for a minute and said, "Well, some are more despicable than others, but that's probably part of what makes them seem human and interesting. Besides," I said, "haven't you ever done anything despicable?" She looked really shocked for a minute, and then we both quickly changed the subject.

I suppose one reason "Mad Men" is popular is that it is easy to feel morally superior to the characters. And I think part of the huge interest in the Bob and Maureen McDonnell trial was the opportunity to hear about the moral failings of a prominent person. These things give us a reason to think well of ourselves. But the fact is, none of us are innocent, at least not in the theological sense. From time to time, ordinary people say or do despicable things. That does not shut the door of God's mercy on us. Elsewhere in Romans, Paul says that God justifies the "ungodly" (5:6), meaning the pagan Gentiles with their unholy ways, who are turning to Jesus Christ. God credits them with righteousness through their faith. You would expect God to credit all the good, righteous people, but Paul says the "ungodly" are also beneficiaries of God's grace – in fact, it was for the sake of the "ungodly" that Jesus Christ came into the world.

When Bob McDonnell left the courthouse on September 4 after the guilty verdict, he was thronged by reporters asking about his reaction to the verdict. "All I can say is my trust remains in the Lord," McDonnell said.[36] This could mean that he still thinks of himself as innocent, not only from a purely legal perspective but that he simply can't see himself as a person who could ever do a

---

[36] "Ex-Va. governor Robert McDonnell guilty of 11 counts of corruption," *The Washington Post*, September 4, 2014, A1.

despicable thing, and believes that God will vindicate him because of his essential righteousness. I prefer to think, though, that as a Christian he knows that he is dealing with a generous God who doesn't deal with us according to our great virtue but according to God's unilateral decision to be merciful to the less-than-righteous.

Who among us is always "on the up and up"? Despicable me, despicable us: we are still descendants of Abraham by faith, children of God and heirs of God's promises, standing not on our own unassailable righteousness but on the righteousness of Jesus Christ.

Grace Presbyterian Church
Springfield, VA
March 1, 2015

No Condemnation
Romans 8: 1-6

Whenever you see the word "therefore" in one of Paul's letters you know that you are coming to the end of a long argument and that Paul is winding up to make his point. In the chapters preceding the verses we just read, Paul has taken his readers through a somewhat complicated thesis on how the law – the Torah, or the law of Moses – while good and holy in itself, has turned out to be a trap for people who want to do the right thing but somehow do the wrong thing, which is pretty much everybody. The problem with the law, Paul says, is that it can't fix human nature, because sin is more powerful than the law. So, the law has a way of turning a simple commandment, like "do not covet," into a temptation – all of a sudden, the very thing you're being told not to do becomes more desirable and attractive. So, in the verses leading up to chapter 8 Paul cries out, speaking for every human being, "I know the law but I still can't keep it! Who will rescue me from this body of death?" The answer Paul is getting to, of course, is Jesus Christ, who snatches us from the domain of sin and death and transfers us to the domain of the Spirit, the place of life and peace.

That is the sense of the larger section that we just read part of, but I want to focus on the first verse: "There is now therefore no condemnation for those who are in Christ Jesus."

"No condemnation": those are astounding words. Where on earth can you go where there is no condemnation? You can't read the paper or turn on the TV without hearing stories of condemnation. The insincere public apology has become a rite of passage for public officials, sports team owners or players, or corporation executives who have been condemned for insensitive or ill-considered remarks. Verbal condemnation is the stock-in-trade for talk-radio hosts – they would have nothing to say if there were not a never-ending supply of misguided politicians, illegal immigrants, unwed mothers, or welfare cheats to condemn on the air.

We have seen how tragedy often brings people together to help and support each other, but condemnation is another, more sinister kind of human glue. For example: I don't claim to know what the U.S. government or the border authorities should do about the Central American children who have tried to enter the U.S. to escape the drug wars in their countries – but I am sickened by the words of condemnation that have brought together the people of some Texas border towns. These children, they say, almost as one voice, are carrying diseases; they are a threat to the community, law-breakers who don't belong here. How those words of condemnation must hurt, how they must cut into the souls of the children who hear them.

Condemnation cuts into souls and bodies. How terrible it is when a whole group is condemned for the actions of a few, as we have seen in the disproportionate violence inflicted on the people of Gaza this past week.

Condemnation, with its often deadly results, is everywhere. It seems to be part of the structure of the world under the law of sin and death.

Fear of condemnation is and always has been a powerful human motivator. Sometimes it is hard to tell whether we try to do the right thing for the love of doing the right thing or so that we won't be caught falling short of expectations: society's, our parents', our peers', our own. The fear of being found out, our behavior and our very *being* held up for inspection and seen as not good enough, not moral enough, not acceptable – we all carry this fear somewhere inside, this fear of condemnation that cuts into our souls.

> • I think of the high-school girl who starts out her day wondering what about her will be "condemned" today: her clothes, the way she wears her hair, the music she listens to, the people she talks to.

> • I think of the mother whose 16-year-old son got caught at school with drugs in his backpack and now, along with her fear for her child, she is afraid to face the other parents at the school – she knows they already condemn her, they're saying she has failed as a parent.

- I think of the man who is at the pinnacle of his career, a whole string of achievements to his credit, who can take no satisfaction in what he has accomplished. He can't see himself as he is, because he haunted by his father's criticism. In his mind, he is still a small boy who has brought home a mediocre report card or failed on the athletic field, condemned by his father's judgment.

- I think of all those people who once ran afoul of the temporal law, and now are lawbreakers forever in the eyes of the justice system. I heard about an elderly woman in Louisiana just a few days ago. She was arrested for shoplifting and because she was caught with one half of a Xanax in her purse two years ago, she's now labeled a repeat offender and is probably looking at five years in prison. She was condemned even before her case got to court.

All this condemnation – whether personal, political, social or legal -- belongs to what Paul calls the law of sin and death. In Paul's eyes, this law is as immutable and inexorable as the law of gravity or the conservation of mass. Condemnation is something we all do, and it is done to all of us.

But now here is Paul saying there is no condemnation for those who are in Christ Jesus. I feel like repeating it over and over, because it sounds too incredible to believe.

A few months ago, I heard a young lawyer tell his story. When he was a somewhat indifferent second-year law student he got sent to talk with prisoners on death row and there he found his vocation, working with the most thoroughly condemned people of all, the ones society has said do not deserve to live. One day this law student informed a man that his sentence would not be carried out in the next year, as the man expected.

"Say that again," the man said.

"Your sentence will not be carried out next year," the student repeated.

"Say that again," the man said.

He wanted to hear the words over and over again: "No condemnation," at least not for another year. It was only a temporary reprieve, not a full pardon, but the convicted man was overjoyed, overwhelmed by this good news he had received.

Paul says to us that in Jesus Christ there is **no condemnation** – that is, there is a full reprieve, the sentence is commuted. The District Attorney, whoever that is for us, has been stripped of his power. Can we hear the joy in that message? Can we imagine what it would feel like not to feel condemned? Not to be constantly picking at ourselves and finding ourselves unacceptable? Not to be constantly worrying about what other people are thinking about us? To honestly acknowledge our faults and failures before God and to know that God accepts us, and that because we are "in Christ," God gives us the opportunity for a fresh start – that God is actually working to transform us through the Spirit of Christ? And knowing all that, to suddenly find that we no longer have the urge to pick at and find fault with other people? That we can say to another person, "you are not condemned"?

I heard about a church that had a banner on their front lawn that said, simply, NO CONDEMNATION. I wonder if more people would come to our churches if we got that message out loud and clear. I know there are people out there who are interested in Jesus, interested in the church, but just don't feel that they would be accepted. Maybe they drink too much or have a history of drug abuse. Maybe they are impoverished single mothers with a history of unstable relationships. Maybe they've done some time in prison. Maybe they've been told that their sexual orientation is sinful. Whatever it is, they feel condemned. One woman with a checkered history was asked about herself by an NPR interviewer: "I know Jesus died for our sins and all that, but I think he died for other people, not for me."

How many people think that about themselves? How many times are we tempted to think that about ourselves, that even the great wide net Jesus Christ has cast throughout the world has failed to catch us? How many of us secretly condemn ourselves, and think that our opinion counts more than God's?

"No condemnation" means that life doesn't have to be an endless cycle of judgment and self-judgment. "No condemnation" means that we can live with more freedom and more joy, more kindness and generosity. "No condemnation" means that God's love is more powerful than the law of sin and death, and that love has the power to transform us and transform the world. Let's hear Paul again: "The law of the Spirit of life in Christ Jesus has set us free from the law of sin and death." You can say that again, and again, and again.

Grace Presbyterian Church
Springfield, VA
July 13, 2014

Mercy in the Face of Chaos, Loss, and Death

When bad things happen to the faithful, what is the appropriate response? What do we do with our fear, and where do we find hope? And how do we live in the face of "the last enemy," death? God does not protect us from pain, loss and suffering, but assures us through the shocks and struggles of our earthly life that nothing may separate us from God's love in Jesus Christ.

"Precious in My Sight"
Isaiah 43:1-7, Luke 3: 21-22

"Do not fear, for I have redeemed you; I have called you by name, you are mine." When God speaks to the exiles of Israel in the text we just read, God is breaking a 50-year silence. To put these words into their historical context: In 587 BC Jerusalem was besieged and then invaded by the Babylonian army. During the time of siege there was chaos in the city and many people starved to death. When the attackers finally broke through the city's defenses, they laid waste to it, burning down everything, including the Temple of Jerusalem. Then they took the king and his family and his court and the priests and the writers and everyone else who had some kind of public role and force-marched them north through the desert to Babylon.

It felt like the end of the world. Certainly, everyone thought it would be the end of the people of God called Israel. Everything was gone: the royal palace, the temple, and the civic structures. The only thing left for the people to do was to assimilate, become part of the Babylonian culture and forget about the past, forget about their former identity. I've read stories about some of the European immigrants who came to this country in the early 20th century, to escape war or famine or political oppression: in most cases, they came without any hope of ever going back home – as indeed may be the case for many of the Syrian refugees today. But in the days before telephones, airplanes and the Internet, an immigrant was often shut off forever from the country and the people who had raised him, cared for him, given him his identity. That's what exile was for the people of Israel, but it was even worse, because they had also been publicly humiliated. The people around them looked down on them and made fun of them. They said, "Where is your God now? It doesn't look like your Yahweh cares much about you."

The exile lasted almost fifty years. Babies were born and a generation grew up that had never known anything but Babylon, and that made the parents and grandparents sad.

But then, into the silence and paralysis of the exile came a word of hope: the prophet Isaiah announced that the international tide had turned, that God was doing something new in the world and was doing it through the king of Persia, who would defeat Babylon and let all the captured people go home. Isaiah announces this stunning good news from God in words of amazing tenderness: "Do not fear, for I have redeemed you; I have called you by name, you are mine." The words "do not fear" are repeated twice in the short passage we read today, and over and over again in the surrounding verses. They seem to be God's favorite words to God's people. In three little chapters, God says these words five times:

> "Do not fear...for I am your God." (41:10)
> "Do not fear, I will help you." (41:13)
> "Do not fear, for I have redeemed you." (43:1)
> "Do not fear, for I am with you." (43:5)
> "Do not fear, or be afraid." (44:8)

In fact, one of the most frequently recurring phrases in the entire Bible is "Fear not," or "Do not be afraid." God says it to Moses and the kings of Israel and the prophets: "Do not be afraid of Pharaoh." "Do not be afraid to face the king of Assyria and his armies." "Do not be afraid of the Babylonians." "Do not be afraid of the people who can curse you and imprison you." It's what Gabriel says to Mary when he tells her she will have a child. Jesus says to his disciples, "Do not be afraid of the storm." "Do not be afraid of the Romans." "Do not be afraid of those who kill the body and after that have no more they can do." "Do not be afraid, little flock, for it is your Father's good pleasure to give you the kingdom." And he says to all of us, "Do not be afraid. I am the first and the last."

The Old Testament scholar Walter Brueggemann has observed that the Bible is much more concerned with the threat of chaos than it is with sin and guilt. That is to say, the Bible speaks to our sense of helplessness even more than it does to our sense of guilt or unworthiness. I think Brueggemann is right. We have been so conditioned by the Protestant Reformation to focus on the Bible's words of forgiveness that we ignore its even more all-encompassing message: "Don't be afraid." You might say that is the central *commandment* of the entire Bible.

When you think about it, that is the assurance we need to hear above all the others, and we don't hear it very often. Consumer culture tells us about all the ways we can fix our fears: how to hedge against a market crash; what kind of homeowners' insurance to get as protection against fire and flood; how to subscribe to an online dating service so we don't have to face being alone, ever. The market has a solution for every kind of fearsome situation. But the underlying message is "Life is actually pretty terrifying – you *should* be afraid." Sellers of consumer products and services are not going to tell us not to be afraid – if we weren't afraid they would have nothing to sell us. They are not the only ones who play to our fears. Many political campaigns are based on exploiting fear: of immigrants, of minorities, of another country getting ahead of us in *anything*, of what the other candidate would do if he or she were elected.

It's possible that some of us, perhaps many of us, have not heard the words "don't be afraid" since our parents said them to us. Maybe we'd had a nightmare and called out in our sleep and they came to comfort us. Maybe we were afraid of monsters lurking in our rooms and our parents would say "don't be afraid, I'm here with you." Or maybe we'd just figured out that the people close to us would die someday, and we would die, and our parents said, "Don't be afraid, nothing like that will happen for a long, long time." Why did we believe these words when our parents said them? Because when they said they'd be there with us, if they were the right kind of parents, we knew they would be. As we grew up we realized that there would be bad things that would happen that they couldn't protect us from, but that they would never abandon us, they would never just leave us to fend for ourselves. We had that assurance because we knew we belonged to them. They said to us what God said to the children of Israel: "You are precious in my sight, and I love you."

Those words may have been echoing in Jesus's head on the day he was baptized. What God said on that day was very similar: "You are my Son, the Beloved; with you I am well pleased." Jesus heard God's voice claiming him, establishing his identity. Maybe Jesus also heard those other words from long ago: "When you pass through the waters, I will be with you; and through the rivers, they shall not overwhelm you; when you walk through fire…the flame shall not consume you."

He needed to keep remembering these words, because the very next thing that happened after his baptism was that he was driven into the wilderness, another place of exile, to be tempted and tested. Through all those forty days of hunger and loneliness, cold nights and scorching midday heat, and the ever-present threat of wild animals, Jesus must have clung to those words: "You are my Son, the Beloved…You are precious in my sight, and I love you."

Every time we baptize a baby or a child or an adult, we are affirming once again these words of God to the children of God: "You are my beloved. You are precious in my sight. When you pass through the waters, I will be with you." And we say prayers for the person being baptized: prayers that God will watch over them and protect them, defend them from evil, and help them to grow in the knowledge and love of Jesus Christ. We say these prayers knowing that there are certain things in life they cannot be protected from. They can't be protected from loss and heartbreak, they can't be protected from certain kinds of failure and disappointment, they can't be fully protected from sickness or injury, and they can't ultimately be protected even from death itself. In other words, they cannot be protected from the human condition.

But they don't have to be afraid. For in our baptism God says to each one of us, "I have redeemed you, you are mine." The way Paul says it is that nothing in all creation, not even the depths of loss or sorrow or sickness or weakness or failure, not even death, will be able to separate us from God's love. John Calvin put it yet another way: "God refuses to be deprived of his rightful possession."

We are God's rightful possession. That is our baptismal assurance. We have been "sealed by the Holy Spirit and marked as Christ's own forever." We are bound to him and he is bound to us, through life and death and life again.

Grace Presbyterian Church
Springfield, VA
January 10, 2016

God of the Living
Luke 20:27-38

A couple of weeks ago, I heard a portion of a radio program about Disney World that I found fascinating. The story included interviews with people who vacationed in Disney World year after year, sometimes several times a year; two of the people interviewed, a woman and her daughter, had moved permanently into the Disney Village. The daughter explained why she'd chosen to live in Disney World year-round; "everyone, everything in this place says to me that I matter."

The Disney Village is an incorporated city. Like any other city, it has houses and apartments, stores and theaters, restaurants and clubs. What it does not have are churches. People in Disney World do not look to God and the Scriptures to let them know that they matter: they look to Mickey and Donald and Goofy, and the whole apparatus of pleasuring the consumer, telling them that their personal likes and dislikes, what makes them smile and relax as well as what makes them nervous and anxious, are of the utmost significance.

Disney World is a place where there are no downers. Everything is upbeat and cheerful. Nothing sad or depressing is permitted in its sunny neighborhoods. There is no dirt or poverty or sickness to be seen. As far as the observer can tell, there is no death in Disney World. Maybe that is the reason there is no place for the church there. The church has always had quite a bit to do with the topic of death.

Disney World is the perfect emblem of a culture that says that thinking about death is morbid and talking about it in bad taste. This perspective is actually something relatively new in human history. Less than a century ago, before there were commercial funeral homes and memorial services instead of funerals, death was a persistent feature of most people's personal landscape. The funeral procession, with a horse-drawn hearse accompanied by dozens of black-clad mourners on foot, was a common sight in every town. People were encouraged to think about their own eventual death and to prepare for it spiritually. Two of America's greatest poets, Emily Dickinson and Walt Whitman, focused much of their writing on envisioning their own deaths.

The New Testament is dominated by thought and talk about death. Death is the unwelcome visitor that stalks through its pages, the "last enemy" still to be conquered after God has put every other enemy underfoot and created a new world order. Death is the enemy that God conquers by means of resurrection.

When the Sadducees come to Jesus to put to him a hypothetical question about resurrection, it is his last week on earth. He is in Jerusalem now, teaching every day in the Temple while the temple authorities plot to kill him. Within a few days of his conversation with the Sadducees he will be arrested and condemned. So, the Sadducees' question about the resurrection is not a hypothetical for Jesus. He is living out his last days, staking everything he has, and is, on God's faithfulness.

The Sadducees are not really interested in what Jesus might have to say about resurrection. They are trying to trap him with a trick question, just as another group of temple authorities had tried to trap him with a question about paying taxes. We don't read nearly as much about the Sadducees as we do about the Pharisees in the Gospels. This is their only appearance in Luke, and they are identified not by what they affirm but by what they deny. They were an elite group in first-century Judaism, the guardians of the Temple; they were often wealthy. They might be described as religious conservatives, while the Pharisees were the progressives. Part of the Pharisees' progressiveness was believing that there would be a general resurrection of the dead – they accepted the later books of what Christians now call the Old Testament, books which spoke explicitly of a resurrection, while the Sadducees' only Bible was the five books of Moses. That's why Jesus quoted Moses back to them in affirming the resurrection: "God is not a God of the dead but of the living, for all are alive in God."

The Sadducees' question about the one bride for seven brothers was based on the ancient custom of levirate marriage, the custom by which the unmarried brother of a man who died without children was obligated to marry the brother's widow. If the brother and the woman then had a son, he would legally be the son of the woman's first husband and the nephew of his biological father. This custom, weird as it sounds to us, served two practical purposes: it kept the family's wealth in the family and it provided protection for the widow, who otherwise would have been destitute. More than that, though, this custom was about how you dealt with the ever-present reality of death. It was essential to have an heir, because that's how you lived on beyond the grave. Your descendants would carry your genes and they would remember you. That was the only kind of immortality you could ever have. So, for all the sarcasm of the Sadducees' question, they must have been as death-haunted as anyone else in their time.

Their question, of course, was not based on any sort of real-life situation: it was deliberately outlandish, designed to ridicule the whole idea of bodily resurrection. Jesus lets them know, quite adroitly and decisively, that their hypothetical string of marriages is in fact irrelevant to the question of resurrection: resurrection life is so qualitatively different from life on earth, with its marriages and divisions of wealth and property, its concerns about who and what belongs to whom, that our categories of earthly life and happiness can't comprehend it. The Sadducees imply that resurrection life, or "heavenly" life, is simply a continuation of what we like best on earth, like a great Disney World in the sky that never closes. Jesus says that resurrection is of a different order of reality altogether. And he leaves it at that – he does not offer details.

To some extent, the Sadducee view was the majority view in Jesus' time, just as it is increasingly the majority view today. It is, after all, eminently reasonable and logical. Things that are dead tend to stay dead. Try arguing for the resurrection in a group of secular friends, and you will see how quickly you run out of things to say, how few arguments you have, none of them based on science, how lame your final words on the subject can feel: "Well, we just have to accept that it is a mystery." Even people who find most of Christianity acceptable, even attractive, tend to stumble over the resurrection. As a matter of fact, the early Christians did, too: a big part of Paul's first letter to the Corinthian church is aimed at addressing the doubts and confusion of the Corinthian Christians on this very matter of the resurrection.

> Listen, I will tell you a mystery! We will not all die, but we will all be changed, in a moment, in the twinkling of an eye, at the last trumpet…the trumpet will sound, and the dead will be raised imperishable…this perishable body must put on imperishability, and this mortal body must put on immortality (1 Cor. 15: 51-53).

I don't know if the Corinthians were any less confused after hearing this, but Paul's point was the same as Jesus's: We cannot describe resurrection by the categories we use to describe even the best kind of life here on earth.

As the Sadducees knew, marriage and children are how we perpetuate our own lives in the world. That is the best we can do if things are left up to us. But God can do more than we can ask or imagine. If there is life after death – which is to say, if there is hope after despair, regeneration after destruction, wholeness after brokenness —it is because, and only because, God creates it. God alone can give life to the dead.

What resurrection means is that you don't stop being part of the life of God just because you die. Death doesn't get in the way of God's care for us. We matter that much to the One who created us. As Paul said in the letter to the Romans, "If we live, we live to the Lord; and if we die, we die to the Lord; so then, whether we live or whether we die, we are the Lord's" (Rom. 14: 8). We belong to the "God of the living," now and forever.

Grace Presbyterian Church
Springfield, VA
November 10, 2013

The Absence of Christ
Luke 24:44-51, Acts 1:1-11

"Most people," says writer Richard Lischer, "imagine that God occupies more of the past than the future."[37] That is to say, God and God's doings seem to be more at home on the ceiling of the Sistine Chapel, or in the remains of a temple, or in ancient manuscripts, than in any situation we can imagine in our own lives. God's last mighty act was the resurrection of Jesus from the dead, but then what was there after that? There was only the church, and the Christians and their doctrines, and their fights over the doctrines, and even wars to determine whose doctrine would win, and with all this messiness and turmoil, sometimes it has been pretty hard, if not next to impossible, to discern where God has been in any of it – if, in fact, God has been there at all. Twenty centuries of Christian history, and what we're most aware of is the *absence* of Christ.

When those disciples stood staring up at the sky as he left them for the last time, they may have been expecting him to come back – in a few days, a few weeks at the most. After all, they had lost him and got him back once before. Maybe there would be yet another act in the drama.

But he didn't come back. The church has been waiting for him for twenty centuries, and all the things we do – our worship, our study, our prayer and our service – are what we've learned to do as we wait for him. They are what we do to manage in his absence. He is in heaven, and we are on earth. But once, in the far distant past, God was here on earth in human flesh, someone you could see and touch and listen to, and now he is not here. Now God, or Jesus, seems more like an absentee landlord, and we are left to muddle through as best we can, which even on our best days is not all that good. Yes, it does seem that "God occupies more of the past than the future" – or, for that matter, the present.

---

[37] Richard Lischer, "I Have Seen the Future," in *Sermons from Duke Chapel*, ed. William H. Willimon (Durham and London: Duke University Press, 2005), 289.

The evangelist Luke, who wrote both the Gospel and the book of Acts, wrote for people who were having a hard time imagining a future with God in it. Luke had no idea that he was writing "Bible stories," and he wasn't writing simply for the sake of posterity. He was writing to offer a strengthening word for the people of his time, which was pretty much like all other times, full of trouble and difficulty. The world as it was when Luke wrote looked pretty hopeless to a lot of people. The reliable world they had grown up with was gone or fading away. The Jews had lost the Temple of Jerusalem, the sign of God's presence with the people. And beyond the Jewish community, in the Gentile world as well, there was growing anxiety and disillusionment.

The Roman Empire was plagued by wars, and there was widespread corruption and mismanagement at various levels of government. I imagine that the prevailing mood in Luke's world was something like the mood on Wall Street after the market crash of last fall, and that has now pervaded the entire country as the global economy implodes. An article in *The New Yorker* last week, entitled "The Death of Kings," speculated about whether the financial crisis is the beginning of the end of "the American experiment."[38]

Under such a pessimistic scenario, it is easy to imagine a future with no prospects – a future without God. All this national pessimism is to say nothing, of course, about people's private catastrophes: the good job that suddenly goes up in smoke, the marriage that can't be saved, the shattering diagnosis. Richard Lischer is right: God seems more at home in Sunday-school watercolors or in the Book of Genesis than in anything that could be happening right now, or next week, or beyond. "Jesus has ascended on high to sit at the right hand of God," we proclaim on this Sunday of the church year, and we proclaim it joyfully, but in truth we are like those disciples watching him disappear into the sky (however that happened) while we have to remain firmly rooted to the earth and its many troubles and sorrows. If we are honest, we would rather have him here with us.

---

[38] Nick Paumgarten, "The Death of Kings," *The New Yorker* (May 18, 2009), 40.

So, we worship and pray and sing hymns as a way of adjusting to his absence, to make it less painful. We've heard a story like a memory, that God once walked the earth among human beings, touched their hurts and healed their wounds, fed them with bread from heaven and offered light for their darkness. And even though we weren't there with those first-century people, the *memory* of him is planted deep within us, a memory we feel as an ache of longing.

As Heidi Neumark has written, "I believe we all passed through the heart of God on our way to where we are.... Presence remembered provokes the wound of absence."[39] And so we stand like those forlorn disciples looking up at the heavens, feeling the pain of absence. Feeling that pain, it is easy to believe that God belongs in the past, not the future. I've sometimes wondered why people in churches tend to be more conservative than people in the general population, and I think it has something to do with a longing for the past, a desire to hold on to what once was and cannot be again. The past, it seems, is where God is most reliably to be found.

Yet not one biblical writer ever says such a thing. Luke's story of the Ascension of Jesus is actually a story about the *future*. Let's look again at what Jesus says in the Gospel to the disciples he is about to leave: "Stay here in the city until you have been clothed with power from on high." And then again in the first chapter of Acts: "You will receive power when the Holy Spirit has come upon you; and you will be my witnesses in Jerusalem, in all Judea and Samaria, and to the ends of the earth."

You will receive power! Jesus went away and left them on their own, but he did not leave them without resources. The power that he promised them was the power that would bind them together as one, and that would send them out into the world as witnesses, to tell a story not just about something God had done in the past, but about something God was doing even now, with them and through them. And here was the really amazing thing: the more they told this story, the more they worshiped and broke bread together, the more they met human need, the more they realized that he was still

---

[39] Heidi B. Neumark, *Breathing Space: A Spiritual Journey in the South Bronx* (Boston: Beacon Press, 2003), 212.

Lisa D. Kenkeremath

with them. And as they went into towns and cities telling their story, they found that his power really was in them. They became fearless; they became eloquent; they became compassionate; they became strong. Everywhere they went, they brought hope and healing and new life to someone, and it was as if Jesus was right there with them after all, just in a different way.

He has been with every generation of the church since then. It is his power, and not the memory of him, that has strengthened Christians to endure sorrow and suffering and loss for centuries, and will continue to do so as long as we gather together to pray the prayers and tell the story, to baptize and make disciples and go into the world. He is with us in our present, and he will be with us in our future – however frightening the future may look to us right now. He has ascended, but he has not abandoned us; he has simply given us what we need to act in his name in a world that is without Christ, and sorely in need of him.

The church is not a memorial society for Jesus. The Spirit of Jesus Christ will not permit us to remain in the past, because the past is not large enough for God. The longing we feel, the ache of missing him, is meant to keep us moving forward, into God's future, a future big enough to include all of us. And the far horizon of that future, which we cannot see but which is God's promise to us, wears the face of Christ, who waits for us, in the place where he has gone ahead of us.

Idylwood Presbyterian Church
Falls Church, VA
May 24, 2009

To Whom Shall We Go?
John 6: 58-69

In all four of the Gospels, Peter is the first one to begin to figure out who Jesus is. In Matthew, Mark, and Luke he boldly announces his discovery: "You are the Messiah." John, as always, tells the story somewhat differently: Peter doesn't identify Jesus as "Messiah," but points to him as the one with the secret to eternal life.

This is the point of no return in the twelve disciples' journey with Jesus. From this time on, they will be inseparable from Jesus, until the time of betrayal and desertion right before his death.

Peter's confession of faith was far from guaranteed. The responses to Jesus up to now have been widely divergent, from complaining and disbelief and rejection to Peter's declaration. Chapter 6 began with an action that was sure to make Jesus popular: He fed a crowd of 5000 people with five loaves of bread and two fish. He then explained that what he was doing was meant not only to help them recall God's feeding of the Israelites with manna in the wilderness, but also to show them that a new kind of divine provision had arrived in Jesus himself. To make sure everyone understood, he has spoken of himself as the "bread that came down from heaven." At least some in the crowd might have been with him on this point, but then he turned them off by telling them that if they really wanted to live they needed to eat his flesh and drink his blood.

That is where our reading picks up today, and it is the make-or-break moment for Jesus and his followers. I need to explain here that there are three categories of people around Jesus at this point in John's Gospel. The largest group is the "crowd," who were probably the kind of people who will show up wherever something interesting seems to be going on but who are not necessarily committed to the person or event on display. The people in the "crowd" may have had the kind of interest in Jesus that you might have for an entertaining street performer – and besides, most people will not turn away from an offer of free food. A smaller group of the people around Jesus John refers to as "disciples" –

these are genuine followers, people who are interested in his works and teaching, who feel compelled to be in his presence, but they are not the same as the "Twelve," Jesus' hand-picked inner circle. It is this middle group of "disciples" that begin to fall away at the end of the events reported in John 6. "This teaching is difficult," they say. "Who can accept it?" When they say it is "difficult," they don't mean that it's hard to understand – they mean that it's offensive, unpalatable, not at all what they hoped or expected to hear. Jesus was creeping them out with all his talk of flesh-eating and blood-drinking.

The thing is, though, Jesus has made the most explicit offer of himself that can be imagined, and his followers react by turning away. Jesus has been used to being rejected by the religious leaders, the Judean officials, but this is something new. The disciples' difficulty, of course, is that when Jesus talks about his "flesh," that's all they see. They don't see the Word made flesh, a human being enlivened through and through by the Spirit of God.

"Because of this," John says – because they don't see this and because Jesus' words are so disturbing – "many of his disciples" – this is the larger circle of followers, not the Twelve – "turned back and no longer went about with him. So Jesus asked the Twelve, 'Do you also wish to go away?'" Can you hear the sadness in that question? Maybe it is my imagination, but I think there is something plaintive in Peter's response, too: "Lord, to whom can we go? You have the words of eternal life. We have come to believe and to know that you are the Holy One of God."

"Lord, to whom can we go?" There is no one else. Following this man Jesus, Peter realizes, is no easy thing. We could all wish for a more congenial, crowd-pleasing, humorous and upbeat sort of messiah, someone who never scares or challenges us, but this is the Messiah we have: someone who talks in such disturbing ways that he drives people away; someone who gets the civil and religious authorities all nervous and jumpy; someone who overturns all our beliefs about what a good life consists of; someone who even makes us rethink what we thought we knew about God – and because of all this, someone who is on a sure path toward arrest, trial, condemnation, and execution.

Is this the person we want to be hanging out with? the Twelve must be asking themselves. Better to get out now, before things get ugly and dangerous.

But there is something else about this man that compels them to stay: he has the words of eternal life. Maybe that is why when they are with him they feel more alive than they do with anyone else. It seems to them that they are being brought in touch with a part of themselves they didn't even know existed, and that at the same time they are truly meeting God, not just hearing about God. They are discovering the depths of their own souls; at the same time, they are more sensitive to what is going on all around them. It's as if every moment is touched with eternity. They are not the people they were before they met Jesus. Their old selves don't fit anymore; their old lives don't fit anymore. They've become used to hearing the words of eternal life, and now every day feels holy and full of mystery and charged with meaning. There is no going back or getting out. This is the one with the words of eternal life. To whom else can they go? To whom else can we go?

There are others, of course, who offer spiritual excitement or spiritual comfort. There are so many others out there, self-help gurus and positive-thinking evangelists and New Age philosophers. There are people who will tell us how to unlock our inner potential to have the life we've always wanted, train our brains to banish all negative thoughts, and tap wellsprings of cosmic energy that can propel us to new levels of achievement and happiness.

I know these kinds of contemporary messiahs are very helpful to a lot of people. I just don't know how helpful they are when you realize that the people you love are going to die, and that you are going to die, and there is nothing any of us can do about it. I don't know how helpful these spiritual guides or life coaches are when you see that everything our bright, loud world counts as valuable is not going to last. Youthful strength and good looks; academic, professional, and athletic achievement; social success; even autonomy to make our own decisions – all of these, eventually, will fall away, and we will be left with ourselves and what we have made of our lives. What will we have with which to face eternity?

A couple of weeks ago, the NPR program "Fresh Air" featured an interview with the actor Frank Langella.[40] It was a wonderful interview – Langella was so honest about himself, without any of the self-congratulation of the celebrity actor, that I found all his responses riveting. He had written a memoir of his life onscreen and onstage, but instead of simply telling the events of his life he focused on telling about other people, mostly actors and directors, who had made an impression on him. He told Terry Gross one story from the book, about an actor named Cameron Mitchell, who, when Langella met him, had had a serious comedown since the days of his success on the stage and screen. He had become a heavy drinker, gained a lot of weight, and was something of a physical and emotional wreck. He and Langella met on the set of a play in which he had been the leading man years ago; Langella was now to play the leading role. Draped across a chair was the jacket Mitchell had worn in the play years ago, now several sizes too small for him. Someone, maybe a director's assistant, picked it up off the chair and coyly gave it to Mitchell. He squeezed himself into the jacket and began dancing and clowning around for the people on the set. Everyone laughed but Langella – he could see how much pain the older actor was in.

Not too many years later Mitchell died, and his name was included among those remembered at the Academy Awards ceremony. Langella noticed how there were great bursts of applause for some of the deceased, but just a tiny ripple of clapping for Mitchell. "Even in death, we are ranked," he mused. And then he realized that he was sitting among a crowd of people who expected the clothes they were wearing that night to fit them forever.

To whom do we go when we realize that the clothes we are wearing now, the life we are living now, will not fit us forever? To whom do we go when we realize that we need something rather more durable to see us through our years of inevitable loss and decline? To whom do we go for the life that will fit us forever, even beyond death itself?

---

[40] Interview by Terry Gross, August 16, 2012.

There is only one who has the words of eternal life, the one the Gospels name as the Messiah, the Christ, the Holy One of God. To whom else *can* we go?

Good Samaritan Presbyterian Church
Waldorf, MD
August 26, 2012

Prison Break
Acts 16: 16-34

We often forget that a significant portion of the New Testament was written from a prison cell. When Paul writes at the end of a letter "remember my chains," he's apologizing to his readers for his bad handwriting: he can't form the letters properly because of the hindrance of manacles and chains. Philippians, Colossians, and the book of Revelation were all written from jail or prison. Elsewhere, in the Gospels and in Acts, we find accounts of beatings, trials, imprisonments and executions that are part of the territory for the people of God. In the Christian world and even outside it, the prison letter has a grave and awesome authority, the witness of someone who is willing to suffer for the justice of God's cause. Think of Bonhoeffer's letters from Tegel prison in Nazi Germany, or Martin Luther King, Jr.'s Letter from a Birmingham Jail. Paul is in that company.

Acts 16 describes the events that lead to Paul's imprisonment in Philippi, along with his co-worker Silas. Since we met them with Lydia in our story last week, Paul and Silas have evidently been in Philippi a while, long enough to get under the skin of the city authorities. The event that gets them in trouble is the exorcism of a "spirit" from an enslaved young girl, thus preventing her holders from making money off her. It's not really clear why Paul was so annoyed at this girl's proclamations – she wasn't really saying anything different from what Paul and Silas had been saying: "We are servants of the Most High God, and we proclaim to you a way of salvation." Maybe Paul was just in a bad mood that day, maybe he was repulsed by the girl's owners, who knows? At any rate, what follows is a nasty little vignette of scapegoating and mob psychology. The slaveholders and then the city authorities whip up the anger of the crowd by presenting the missionaries (who happen to be Roman citizens) as dangerous outsiders and threats to the Roman way of life.

First-century prisons were about as bad as a prison can be. They were often packed beyond capacity, especially in times of war or civil disturbances. Heat and dehydration would have been the most usual consequences of this overcrowding, along with the spread of disease. The prisons were generally windowless, without light or ventilation. Prisoners were dependent on family members and friends – or in the case of the early Christians, the church – to provide their food, bedding, and clothing. Chains and manacles were often used, and sometimes the prisoners were chained together. The weight of the chains was so debilitating that after a while the prisoner's limbs would atrophy. Paul and Silas were thrown into an "inner cell," which means they would have been in complete darkness both day and night.

In the current controversy over whether the Guantanamo Bay military prison should be closed or remain in operation, there have been debates over whether conditions there are better or worse than in a Supermax prison on the U.S. mainland. Neither one is as horrible as a first-century prison. Still, one fact doesn't change: imprisonment is an assault on the human spirit. In the case of Paul and Silas, they were denied due process, stripped of their clothing and beaten. They were hurt and humiliated. Yet in the prison they were praying and singing hymns. There was something in them that could not be imprisoned.

Although Paul would do significant prison time at a later date, this incarceration, mercifully, was a brief one, with a spectacular ending: an earthquake, which blasted open the prison doors and broke the chains of the prisoners. This solid fortress, a concrete physical expression of human systems of control, has been shaken to the foundations.

As it turns out, the prisoners are not the only ones who are set free. The jailer, who was ready to kill himself rather than suffer the shame of being derelict in his duty, is amazed to see that the prisoners have not run away. Realizing that something has happened that defies explanation, he falls down before Paul and Silas: "What must I do to be saved?" The answer is what it always is in the book of Acts: "Repent. Be baptized. Receive the Holy Spirit and start to live in a new way." So, the jailer leads Paul and Silas out of the jail, cleans and soothes their wounds, and is baptized along with his household. They have joined Lydia and her household as new members of First Church, Philippi. No less than the people he formerly held in chains, this jailer has been released, set free for a completely different kind of life.

The New Testament prison stories are not just about literal captivity. In this story, the people most in need of salvation are the people outside the prison cells: the jailer, the cynical and mercenary slaveholders, and the angry and vicious townspeople.

It's still true that you don't have to be inside a prison cell to be in chains, to be in a dark, airless, hopeless-feeling place. There are prisons of our own making.

There is the man who is so angry at someone in his family, someone he had a falling-out with a long time ago, that it consumes his life. His hurt and anger have become a protective shell that keeps him at arm's length from other people, people who could hurt him again if he let his guard down. He is safe, he thinks, but deep inside he's one of the loneliest people on earth. He would like to forgive and be set free from this prison, but he doesn't know how.

There is the woman who has a dream of perfection. She's a success at her job, she's a loving mother and wife, she has a beautiful house that is always clean, she's always well-dressed and well-mannered. Her children's parties are always the most clever, the most well-planned and executed. People think well of her, but she doesn't think well of herself. She looks around at what she has achieved and thinks, it's not good enough. I could do better. With everything she accomplishes, she's satisfied for a few minutes, but then she's unhappy again. She doesn't understand what is wrong with her.

There is the teenager who can't settle for anything less than all A's and as many AP courses as the school allows him to take. He's succeeding at all his goals, and his parents are thrilled. They won't let him consider anything less than a top college, but he's not so sure that's what he wants. He's tired all the time, way too tired for a sixteen-year-old, and he feels empty inside. Sixteen years old, and life is no fun. He knows what his parents want, but he doesn't know what he wants.

There is another teenager who wants desperately to go to college, but no one in her family or neighborhood has ever done that. She studies hard, but her parents don't have the money to send her to college, and the kids in her neighborhood are always telling her that her hard work is a waste of time. You won't get out of here, they say, no matter how smart you are. She is beginning to believe them.

What must *they* do to be saved – to be released from these places of captivity? What must *we* do to be set free from the prison fortresses we build for ourselves, or allow others to build for us?

"Believe in the Lord Jesus," Paul said. I don't know if the people described above would be convinced. It sounds pretty simplistic. In the book of Acts, people profess belief in Jesus and are baptized, and all their troubles seem to melt away. We know it's not quite that simple. After all, believing in Jesus made life a lot harder for Paul and Silas. But how about this:

Believe that you are lovable for who you are, not for what you can do.
Believe that you are not the sum total of your bad experiences, and they are not what define you.
Believe that who you are and what you are worth does not depend on being perfect, or being right, or being what other people want you to be.
Believe that God's will and desire for every human being is to live in freedom from the burden of guilt, the burden of anger, the burden of hopelessness, the burden of too-high or too-low expectations of ourselves.
Believe that God sent Jesus for the express purpose of breaking down the prison walls of all that would keep human beings separated from God and each other.
Believe that God sent Jesus to shake the foundations of all that would keep us from life and peace, peace with others and peace within ourselves.

Divine love breaches all the prison walls. Believe this, and you will be saved.

Grace Presbyterian Church
Springfield, VA
May 12, 2013

The Wideness of God's Mercy: The Question of Universalism

God is revealed in Jesus Christ and in Scripture as one whose love for the world is limitless. What does this say about the ultimate fate of nonbelievers? The Bible doesn't speak entirely in one voice on this, and even John's Gospel, which focuses so much on belief in Jesus as necessary for salvation, leaves room for a generous view toward those who have not confessed him as Lord.

"This Is How God Loved the World"
John 3: 1-17

Those of you who follow the lectionary know that we are now in a Matthew year: starting on the first Sunday of Advent 2013 and continuing up to the first Sunday of Advent 2014, the lectionary gives us a reading from Matthew every Sunday – except during Lent. During Lent, we take a break from whatever the appointed Gospel is – Matthew, Mark, or Luke – and read from the Gospel of John.

To move from Matthew to John, as we are doing this year, is to enter a different theological world. In Matthew, we see Jesus as the authoritative teacher of the Sermon on the Mount, and his disciples are those who do what he says, or try to do what he says. For Matthew's Jesus, belief without obedience is meaningless. "Not everyone who says to me, 'Lord, Lord,' will enter the kingdom of heaven, but only the one who does the will of my Father in heaven," Jesus says to his followers in Matthew (7: 21). Matthew is also the only Gospel in which Jesus tells the Parable of the Sheep and the Goats, that sobering story in which the sheep, the ones who will sit at his right hand in the kingdom of heaven, are not necessarily the ones who have professed belief in him or devotion to him – they are the ones who have fed the hungry, clothed the naked, visited prisoners and welcomed strangers. In other words, Matthew's Jesus says, I'm more interested in what you *do* that shows you are following me than in your profession of belief in me.

In John, though, it's all about belief. For John, the world is divided into those who believe in Jesus as the divine Son of God and those who do not. The division is a tragic one. Those who do not believe, John says, "love darkness rather than light"; they are lawless and evil. The world outside the community of believers is a dark, chaotic, ignorant place, populated by the enemies of God and God's Son. Believers are commanded to love each other, as Jesus has loved them – but they are not commanded to actively love those outside the community. Much of the energy of this Gospel comes from Jesus' conflict with unbelievers: The Gospel often has the feel of a long, bitter trial in a law court. Those on trial are the ones who fail to see or refuse to see Jesus for who he is.

Nicodemus, whose story we just read, is one of those on trial. He is the first person in the Gospel to seek Jesus out and question him. It is customary to say that Nicodemus came at night because he was afraid of being seen talking to Jesus. Jesus had already acquired a reputation in Jerusalem as a troublemaker by thundering into the Temple courtyard, brandishing a whip and knocking over tables. It's reasonable to assume that Nicodemus, a man respected at the Temple and in the city, would not want to be seen associating with a radical like Jesus. However, it may not be fair to say that Nicodemus was afraid. Maybe Jesus had gotten Nicodemus so upset that he couldn't sleep, so he went out at night to find Jesus and ask him to give an accounting of himself. Maybe Nicodemus sensed that there was something about Jesus that he had to know more about, something that both disturbed him and excited him, and he couldn't let go of it.

What Nicodemus did seem to be afraid of was the mystery that was Jesus himself. Nicodemus may have been looking for another rabbi like himself, a religious scholar, and what he got instead was someone whose teaching was so strange, so provocative it was threatening.

Nicodemus, we learn, was first attracted to Jesus by the miracles, or "signs" he was performing, and he seems to be focusing on these "signs" when he comes to see Jesus. Nicodemus, in spite of his own high standing as a leader of the Pharisees, a religious expert, comes to Jesus as a genuine seeker. But Jesus immediately throws him off guard with his strange words: "No one can see the kingdom of God without being born from above" (or "born again" – the same Greek word has both meanings). With these words of Jesus, Nicodemus finds the theological ground under his feet shifting uncomfortably, and loses his footing.

Nicodemus is fascinated by Jesus, but he doesn't really "get" him. Nicodemus is a smart, learned man, but with Jesus he's the guy who doesn't get the joke, doesn't understand the play on words. Jesus is a poet, and Nicodemus is almost comically literal-minded.

From a human and literal point of view, Nicodemus is right in what he says – you can't be born all over again. You can't go back in the womb and you can't simply erase the genes, habits, and experiences that have made you who you are. Some psychologists say that people's personalities are pretty well fixed by young adulthood, and that personality will determine the choices they make from here on out. So, biology and psychology seem to rule out the possibility of being "born again."

Nicodemus's problem, of course, is that he looks at Jesus from a purely human point of view. That's why he misses what he's all about. To him, Jesus is an impressive teacher and miracle-worker, but not the Word made flesh.

So, Nicodemus goes away without demonstrating any faith or understanding. He is one of many in the Gospel who doesn't pass the test, who misses the boat on the gift of new life Jesus offers. But the Gospel's verdict on him is not entirely clear, because Nicodemus reappears later, first to defend Jesus's right to a fair trial before a religious tribunal and then to go with Joseph of Arimathea to prepare Jesus's body for burial. Maybe the mystery of Jesus slowly seeped into Nicodemus's consciousness, leading him to faith in a gradual way.

For now, though, Nicodemus has not forsaken his alliance with the world John calls dark and evil. He stands with those in John's Gospel who do not believe and therefore are condemned.

Every Christian has to decide for him- or herself on the matter of whether God's love and grace will ultimately extend even to those who do not profess belief in Jesus Christ. John states quite clearly that those who "will not perish" are those who do believe in Jesus. But the story of Nicodemus and his fumbling after faith seems to me to be more open-ended than that. Nicodemus flunks his face-to-face encounter with Jesus, yet he keeps coming back. He, along with Joseph of Arimathea, is the last person to see and touch Jesus' earthly body above ground. What emotions did he have as the two men carried out this somber task? Was he filled with regret for an opportunity wasted, never to come again? Was Nicodemus, by his failure, doomed to the world of darkness John so grimly describes?

Or was he a person still in process, gracefully given time to sort things out? The Gospel doesn't tell us.

I confess that John is the Gospel I struggle with the most. The contrasts between darkness and light, spirit and flesh, believers and unbelievers, are so starkly drawn that there seems to be no room for the gray areas in which most of us live, where sometimes we make compromises to get by in the world, where we meet good and decent people who belong to other faiths or no faith, and where faithful people come to very different conclusions about what is right and what is wrong, what is true or untrue. John's absolute certainty, his refusal to admit a gray area or to entertain another point of view, can be hard to accommodate in the pluralistic world we live in.

Our concerns about the gospel making sense to a religiously pluralistic world were not John's concerns. What John wants to say – and he says it better than anyone else -- is that you can't make a halfway decision for Jesus Christ. Jesus wants all of us, the whole person, and he won't settle for anything less. Nicodemus was not ready to take that plunge, to submit himself to the complete reorientation of life that is entailed in being "born from above." That was his failure and perhaps his tragedy.

It must also be said that none of the New Testament writers would ever accept the New Age-y claim that "we all believe in the same God, so it doesn't matter what you believe." In Jesus Christ, God encounters us in a distinctly personal, and person-to-person, way. Jesus Christ is not God in the abstract, or God as a religious ideal, or God as the composite of humankind's best thoughts about truth and morality. Jesus comes to us with a specificity that we can't reduce or distill into an "essence" of all faiths. And what Jesus Christ has done in his extraordinary life and unrepeatable death is to show us the specific nature of God's love: "*This* is how God loved the world, by sending God's only Son."

A translational note is in order here. Most of our translations of John 3:16, possibly the most famous verse in the New Testament, say "God so loved the world that he sent his only Son." In this translation, it can sound like Jesus is describing the degree of God's love for the world: "God loved the world *so much* that…". But a more literal translation of the Greek reads "Thus God loved the world," or "In this way God loved the world," or "This is how God loved the world, that he sent his only son." Out of love, God took on human flesh and entered the world we know -- this messy, ambiguous world, in which good and evil, beauty and ugliness, truth and lies, don't just exist side-by-side but often bleed into each other. Because of this, we can say that God's love for the world is total and comprehensive. It doesn't stop at our belief or lack of it. This ignorant, resisting world, this world that John sees as stubbornly and sinfully opposed to God and everything godly, is the world God has loved.

That says to me that no one is truly outside the scope of that love. When Jesus died on the cross, he died loving his enemies – God's enemies – as much as his friends. His resurrection was God's definitive "no" to the evil in the world, God's promise of its eventual defeat. In Jesus Christ God has been revealed as One whose love for the world is limitless. We cannot presume to know where or if resistance to that love is conclusive for all time. All we can do is affirm with John what we do know: that "God did not send Jesus Christ into the world to condemn the world, but so that the world might be saved through him." This is how God has loved, and does love, the world.

Grace Presbyterian Church
Springfield, VA
March 16, 2014

www.ingramcontent.com/pod-product-compliance
Lightning Source LLC
Chambersburg PA
CBHW052150110526
44591CB00012B/1927